NEW YORK 1776

The Continentals' first battle

CAMPAIGN • 192

NEW YORK 1776

The Continentals' first battle

DAVID SMITH

ILLUSTRATED BY GRAHAM TURNER

Series editors Marcus Cowper and Nikolai Bogdanovic

First published in Great Britain in 2008 by Osprey Publishing,
PO Box 883, Oxford, OX1 9PL, UK
PO Box 3985, New York, NY 10185-3985, USA
Email: info@ospreypublishing.com

Osprey Publishing is part of the Osprey Group.

© 2008 Osprey Publishing Ltd.

Transferred to digital print on demand 2013

First published 2008
3rd impression 2010

Printed and bound in Great Britain

A CIP catalog record for this book is available from the
British Library.

ISBN: 978 1 84603 285 1
PDF eBook ISBN: 978 1 84603 840 2
ePub ISBN: 978 1 78200 443 1

Editorial by Ilios Publishing Ltd, Oxford, UK
(www.iliospublishing.com)
Page layout by The Black Spot
Index by Glyn Sutcliffe
Maps by The Map Studio Ltd
3D bird's-eye views by The Black Spot
Battlescene illustrations by Graham Turner
Typeset in Sabon and Myriad Pro
Originated by United Graphic Pte Ltd.

The Woodland Trust
Osprey Publishing is supporting the Woodland Trust, the UK's
leading woodland conservation charity, by funding the
dedication of trees.

www.ospreypublishing.com

Author's dedication
This book is dedicated to my wife, Shirley, and our two sons,
Harry and Joshua.

Artist's note
Readers may care to note that the original paintings from which
the colour plates in this book were prepared are available for
private sale. All reproduction copyright whatsoever is retained
by the Publishers. All enquiries should be addressed to:

Graham Turner
PO Box 568
Aylesbury
Buckinghamshire
HP17 8ZK
UK

www.studio88.co.uk

The Publishers regret that they can enter into no
correspondence upon this matter.

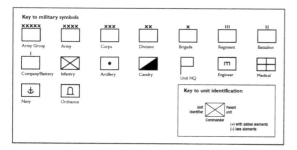

CONTENTS

North America, 1776

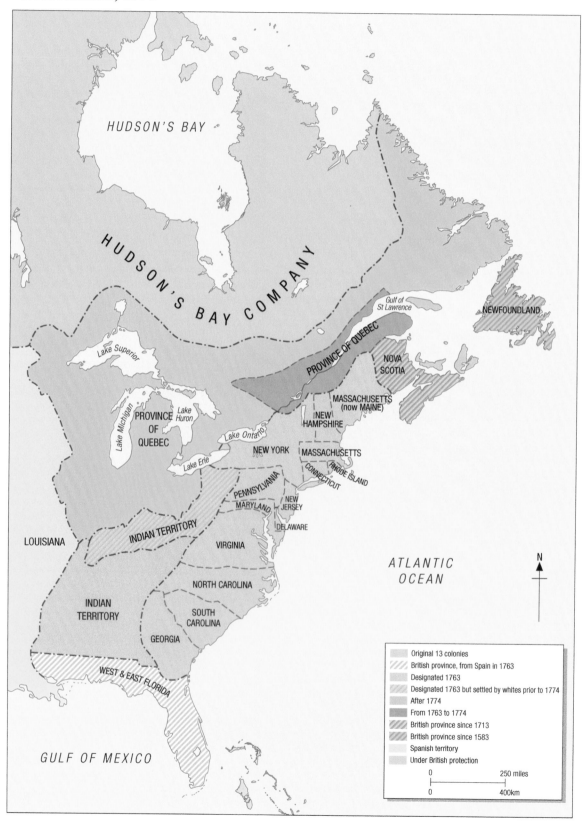

HUDSON'S BAY

HUDSON'S BAY COMPANY

Lake Superior

NEWFOUNDLAND

Gulf of St Lawrence

PROVINCE OF QUEBEC

NOVA SCOTIA

PROVINCE OF QUEBEC

Lake Michigan

Lake Huron

Lake Ontario

Lake Erie

MASSACHUSETTS (now MAINE)

NEW HAMPSHIRE

NEW YORK

MASSACHUSETTS

RHODE ISLAND

CONNECTICUT

PENNSYLVANIA

MARYLAND

NEW JERSEY

DELAWARE

LOUISIANA

INDIAN TERRITORY

VIRGINIA

NORTH CAROLINA

ATLANTIC OCEAN

N

INDIAN TERRITORY

SOUTH CAROLINA

GEORGIA

WEST & EAST FLORIDA

GULF OF MEXICO

	Original 13 colonies
	British province, from Spain in 1763
	Designated 1763
	Designated 1763 but settled by whites prior to 1774
	After 1774
	From 1763 to 1774
	British province since 1713
	British province since 1583
	Spanish territory
	Under British protection

0   250 miles

0   400km

ORIGINS OF THE CAMPAIGN

As British regulars were sent reeling down Breed's Hill for the second time on June 17, 1775, it was no longer possible to pretend that a state of war did not exist between the mother country and her colonies. A scraped-together rebel army, ensconced behind strong fortifications, was inflicting over 1,000 casualties on the redcoats under Major-General William Howe, an appalling casualty rate. Ominously for the British, the Americans were standing firm in the face of massed ranks of professional troops, troops that may have expected to overawe their amateur opponents easily. Ominous for the Americans, of course, was the fact that the British returned for a third advance up the sides of Breed's Hill and, with the Americans running out of ammunition, finally broke through to take the position.

As Howe reflected on his victory (his report showed clearly what he thought: "when I look to the consequences of it, in the loss of so many brave officers, I do it with horror—the success is too dearly bought"), the Americans must also have had mixed emotions. They had performed admirably in their first major engagement with regulars, but the determination of the British was frighteningly clear.

Bunker Hill had shown what the Americans could do if given the benefit of a strong defensive position, but early in the war Washington had no confidence in their abilities in the open field. (Domenick D'Andrea)

"The Horse America throwing his Master." King George III is depicted as a hapless rider losing control of his mount. The "Horse America" looks full of fight and is not taking kindly to the bayonets, swords and hatchets with which the king is trying to subdue it. (LOC, LC-USZ62-1521)

It had been a bad year for the king's troops in the 13 colonies. "The shot heard round the world" had been fired just two months previously. A minor skirmish and harassed withdrawal at Lexington and Concord had now evolved into a siege at Boston, with the impertinent rebels closing in and British commanders and politicians finally realizing that this was no brief uprising to be quelled at the first appearance of substantial numbers of soldiers. In July Lord North wrote to the King, admitting that: "the war is now grown to such a height, that it must be treated as a foreign war. …"

This raised the question of how the colonists could be brought back into the fold. This was not yet a war for independence. Rebel leaders merely wanted their rights as British subjects, as they saw themselves, to be respected. Whether a reconciliation could have been effected by a few simple concessions is an interesting point to debate, but the fact is that Britain chose to exert military force to bring the colonists back to their senses. Contrary to popular myth, the British did not believe they would simply roll over any resistance the colonists could offer. Experienced commanders knew that the vastness of the continent would work against them, as would the huge distances involved in providing and supplying a sizable armed force to operate in North America. Many officers and men had experience of fighting in the French and Indian War and were aware that warfare here was often very different from the large-scale affairs of European conflicts. Adjutant General Harvey commented that "Taking America as it at present stands, it is impossible to conquer it with our British Army. … To attempt to conquer it internally by our land force is as wild an idea as ever controverted common sense."

Howe himself saw Bunker Hill (as the engagement at Breed's Hill was to be remembered) as a blueprint for the failure of the British. From fortified positions the Americans could fight a defensive war to sap the strength of their opponents gradually. Refusing to be drawn into open engagements, they could force the British to attack prepared works and "in this defensive mode, (the whole country coming into them upon every action) they must in the end get the better of our small numbers."

The latter part of Howe's assessment may surprise some, but it demonstrates his awareness not only of the size of the British Army at the

The "battle" of Lexington. As George F. Scheer and Hugh F. Rankin state, "The day of Lexington and Concord marked the transition from intellectual to armed rebellion." (LOC, LC-DIG-ppmsca-05478)

LEFT
This political cartoon from 1775 shows the twin horses of Pride and Obstinacy carrying George III over a precipice, trampling the Constitution and Magna Carta at the same time. (LOC, LC-USZ62-12302)

time (small by the standards of the day) but also of the difficulty involved in getting men to the colonies. In the war that was about to be waged, the burden of attaining victory was to lie squarely on Britain. The colonies merely had to avoid defeat.

The first step in defeating the rebels would involve a shift of base. Besieged in Boston, Howe (who was appointed commander-in-chief of British forces in October 1775) could do nothing and was simply awaiting enough transports to move his army to the starting point for the 1776 campaign: New York. The move south would bring the British into an area of strong Loyalist support and enable the initiation of a new strategy, which involved the deceptively simple process of cutting the colonies in two along the Hudson River, thus dividing militant New England from the source of its supplies, the middle and southern colonies. Two British armies would undertake the work—one, led by Howe, pushing up the Hudson from New York, the second, under Major-General Sir Guy Carleton, moving down the Hudson from Canada.

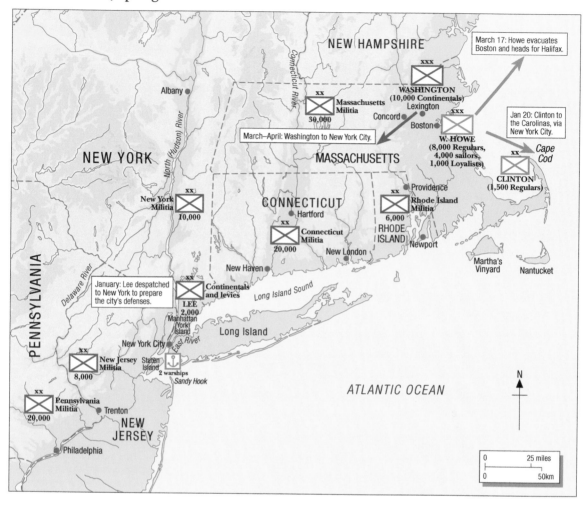

Delays in gathering transport vessels saw 1775 turn into 1776 and the rebels around Boston become the Continental Army, whose commander had no intention of giving the besieged regulars an easy time. General George Washington, aware of the limited experience of his men (and having a fairly low opinion of them) was keen to see them "seasoned" by battle. "The men must be brought to face danger," he reasoned, and although this was a perfectly sensible attitude it was also Howe's dearest hope—had the Americans left "those strong entrenchments, to which alone they may attribute their present security," he might have been able to rout them.

Washington, though he was to make many mistakes as commander-in-chief, did not do so here, preferring to put further pressure on the British (and invite them to try their hand at another Bunker Hill) by fortifying the Dorchester Heights, overlooking Boston. The arrival of Henry Knox's "noble train of artillery" from Fort Ticonderoga made this a possibility and, unable to ignore such a move, Howe prepared to attack on March 5. Bad weather prevented him from carrying out the assault and by the time it had cleared the American defensive works were complete—Howe had no intention of attacking now. Washington then tightened the noose, commencing works on Nook's Hill, even closer to Boston, and rendering Howe's position untenable.

George Washington takes command of the American Army at Cambridge and a legend is born. From a painting by M. A. Wageman. (NA, 148-GW-l78)

On March 17, in some disorganization and with only 78 transport ships available, Howe evacuated his army from Boston, leaving behind a large quantity of supplies and 79 horses. The hasty departure rendered Howe's army ill equipped for a smooth transfer to New York, so he settled on Halifax as a suitable place to regroup and await re-supply and reinforcements.

It had been an undignified evacuation, more than a little embarrassing, and things were also going wrong for the British elsewhere, in the form of the shambolic Charleston Expedition. Limited military manpower had served to heighten an appreciation for loyal elements in the colonies to unrealistic levels. The appearance of redcoats in key areas was expected to provoke Loyalist uprisings that would quickly restore order to entire colonies. The idea was strengthened by communications from various southern Governors. Governor Martin of North Carolina, from the comfort of a British warship at Cape Fear, declared that he could quickly bring his colony to heel with a small force of regulars and the numerous Loyalists who were just waiting for some support. Lord Dunmore requested a very reasonable 200 to 300 men to subdue Virginia, while Lord William Campbell was convinced that 2,000 regulars would bring not only South Carolina to its senses, but also neighboring Georgia.

The temptation to take such assurances at face value was huge and there was also a desire to do *something* while Howe sat and waited in Boston. George III himself was certainly in favor of such limited expeditions: "Every means of distressing America must meet with my concurrence," he commented, "as it tends to bringing them to feel the necessity of returning to their Duty."

North Carolina was chosen as the most likely area to prove receptive and 10,000 stands of arms were sent to the Loyalists there. A force of around 2,000 redcoats, under Henry Clinton, would join them and together they would take control of the colony. Disastrously, the Loyalists rose up at the end of February, when they expected the British to arrive, and were thoroughly beaten by the rebels on February 27 at Moore's Creek Bridge. When Clinton arrived in March, the fleet that should have been waiting for him had still not yet arrived—the first ships would not appear until April and the fleet was not complete until May 31. Clinton, his timetable shattered and his expected Loyalist allies in disarray, probably should have headed straight back to Howe in preparation for the New York campaign. Instead, he tried to rescue something from the situation and launched an attack on Sullivan's Island at the entrance to Charleston Harbor.

The attack was a complete failure, as the landing place chosen for the infantry proved to be unsuitable and the soldiers were unable to support Sir Peter Parker's naval assault. A futile exchange of shot with the defenders of Fort Sullivan saw Parker lose a frigate, and the expedition headed back to Halifax having accomplished nothing.

There had been no turnaround in military fortunes for the British in the early exchanges of 1776, then, but plans were already in motion for a major offensive, one that might even end hostilities in a single campaign. Of paramount importance now was the amassing of a force sufficient to carry out the plans for the 1776 campaign. On reaching Halifax, Howe wrote to the Colonial Secretary, Lord Germain (who had taken over from Lord Dartmouth on November 9, 1775), stating his intention to take New York as soon as he had re-supplied his small army. Intelligence informed Howe that the Americans were fortifying the city. Washington had dispatched Major-General Charles Lee to New York back in January, believing it to be the likely object of Britain's interest in the following campaign, and he had started to send troops to New York as soon as Howe evacuated Boston. The plans Lee drew up (while struggling with a nasty flare-up of gout) included a battery on the Brooklyn Heights to command the East River, with a string of entrenchments and redoubts to protect them from an assault from that direction.

The idea of the Americans constructing organized defensive works must have caused Howe some concern given his experience at Bunker Hill. It also lessened the opportunity for attaining a decisive victory, because Howe had repeatedly stated that he had no intention of storming properly prepared defenses, aware as he was of the difficulty of getting reinforcements if an attack should prove costly. Howe believed that the Americans were actually planning to be more aggressive than he had originally thought. Reports led him to believe they would "try an active war" and he hoped that a touch of overconfidence following Bunker Hill might embolden them to fight in the open, which would give him the opportunity to score his decisive victory, "than which nothing is more to be desired or sought by us, as the most effectual means to terminate this expensive war."

The failed attack on Fort Sullivan was doomed from the start—the fleet that was to join up with Clinton was scattered by a gale soon after leaving Cork and took almost three months to cross the Atlantic. By then, the Loyalist forces in North Carolina had been crushed. (LOC, LC-USZ62-33995)

Halifax (depicted here as it appeared in 1781) gave William Howe the safe haven he needed to reorganize his forces following the unseemly withdrawal from Boston. (LOC, LC-USZ62-34798)

The desire to give the Americans a sharp lesson in the realities of warfare depended on moving quickly. The longer the rebels had to entrench, the less likely an assault would be to rout them and they would have the opportunity to "spin out the campaign if possible without exposing themselves to any decisive stroke."

By June 7, Howe's troops were preparing to sail from Halifax for Long Island with the goal of securing the Brooklyn Heights. At this point, however, Howe's intentions began to waver and his communications with Germain took on a hazy, imprecise tone. Although still promising to seek out battle with the rebels, he restated that this must be on his terms. "Should the enemy offer battle in the open field," he wrote, "we must not decline it, …" but he continued to say that victory in such a battle would be "obtained and prosecuted immediately upon the arrival of the reinforcements."

Was Howe now intending to move only when reinforcements arrived? Such a delay might prove critical, but at least fresh troops from Britain began to arrive the very next day, with the first of Fraser's Highlanders reaching Halifax on June 8. Taking the time to commit to paper his "utter amazement" at the efforts made by Germain, Howe set sail from Halifax on June 11. His army numbered 9,000.

CHRONOLOGY

1775
June 16   Washington appointed commander-in-chief of Continental Army.

June 17   Battle of Bunker (Breed's) Hill.

1776
February 27   Defeat of Loyalists at Moore's Creek Bridge, North Carolina.

March 17   British forces evacuate Boston—Howe is forced to go to Halifax first to reorganize his army.

June 28   The British attack on Fort Sullivan, part of Henry Clinton's Charleston Expedition, fails.

The campaign, June 11–December 14
June 11   Howe sails from Halifax with an army of 9,000, landing at Staten Island.

July 12   The *Phoenix* and *Rose* sail up the Hudson River to test American defenses.

August 1   Clinton rejoins Howe after the Charleston Expedition.

August 22   British forces land on Long Island.

August 27   Battle of Long Island. Howe outflanks the American defenses to score a major victory, but refuses to follow up with an assault on the main lines.

August 29   Washington evacuates American forces from Long Island.

September 15   British forces land on Manhattan Island, at Kip's Bay. Around 3,500 Americans still in New York City escape after British troops fail to advance across Manhattan.

September 16   The British occupy New York City.

September 16   Battle of Harlem Heights. An extended skirmish boosts American morale as British light infantry and the Black Watch are forced to retreat.

September 21   A serious fire sweeps through New York, destroying a quarter of the city.

October 12   Howe lands his army at Throg's Neck but is unable to advance inland.

October 18   The British re-embark and move to Pell's Point. In the battle of Pelham a small force of Americans again prevent the British from quickly moving inland.

October 28   Battle of White Plains. Howe captures a key hill to the right of the American defenses but once more declines to push forward into an all-out assault.

November 16   Fort Washington falls to a combined British–Hessian force, with the loss of more than 2,700 men and a large quantity of supplies.

November 20   Fort Lee is captured, again with a large quantity of supplies and cannons.

November 21 to December 8   Washington is pursued across New Jersey as his army dwindles. Desertions and expiring enlistments see his numbers drop to around 3,500 and he crosses the Delaware into Pennsylvania on December 8.

December 8   British capture Newport, Rhode Island.

Aftermath
December 25/26   Battle of Trenton. Washington delivers a small but crucial victory for the American cause, ending the year on a high note.

1777
January 3/4   Battle of Princeton. Washington takes an even bigger risk at Princeton and again secures a morale-boosting victory.

July 2–4   Burgoyne takes Ticonderoga.

August 16   Battle of Bennington.

September 11   Battle of Brandywine.

September 19   First battle of Saratoga.

September 23   Howe occupies Philadelphia.

October 7   Second battle of Saratoga.

October 16   Burgoyne surrenders.

1778
March 13   France declares war on Great Britain.

1783
November 25   American troops enter New York.

OPPOSING COMMANDERS

BRITISH

General William Howe

There can be few more perplexing characters in British military history than William Howe. Brave, successful, dynamic, he appeared to be everything the British needed to prosecute the war with the rebellious colonies, yet his performance was so patchy that some have even questioned whether he actually wanted to win.

Howe first caught the attention of his superiors in 1758, when he earned praise from James Wolfe for his leadership of the 58th Regiment at Louisbourg. The following year he led the "forlorn hope" onto the Heights of Abraham, helping to take Quebec in the battle that saw Wolfe killed.

The death of his esteemed elder brother, George Augustus Howe, at Ticonderoga in 1758 was a huge blow, and the fact that £250 was donated by the commonwealth of Massachusetts to pay for a monument to George at Westminster Abbey added to Howe's affection for the colonists. As member of parliament for Nottingham, Howe was a critic of the government's policy toward the colonies and on his decision to take up a command in America he said "My going thither was not of my seeking. I was ordered, and could not refuse…"—hardly the most positive frame of mind in which to embark upon a military campaign.

Having led the assault on Bunker Hill with great courage, he was given the local rank of a full general in January 1776 and took over from Thomas Gage as commander-in-chief of British forces in the 13 colonies. Following the 1776 campaign, Howe was knighted, but the 1777 campaign was to prove disappointing, as he failed to defeat the Continental Army decisively and abandoned all ideas of linking up with John Burgoyne, moving southward from Canada along the Hudson as his part of the "Hudson strategy." Successes for Howe at Brandywine, Germantown and Fort Mifflin, as well as the capture of Philadelphia, were nullified by Burgoyne's defeat at Saratoga. Howe resigned in 1778 and returned home, his military career at an end.

Admiral Lord Richard Howe

Having joined the Royal Navy at the age of 14, Richard Howe progressed through a combination of ability and royal influence. He took the Irish title of Viscount Howe on the death of his older brother, George, on July 6, 1758, and by December 1775 he was a vice-admiral.

General William Howe (1729–1814). Howe was the youngest of three brothers and acquired a reputation as a bold, even reckless soldier. His bravery was never in doubt, although his command of the British Army in America would lead many to question his motives. (LOC, LC-USZ62-361 6)

Admiral Lord Richard Howe (1726–99). Richard Howe was reluctant to take command of the fleet in America and insisted upon being made a peace commissioner as well, but in this capacity he was to encounter only disappointment and failure. (LOC, LC-USZ62-45254)

Lieutenant-General Henry Clinton (1730–95). A self-professed "shy bitch," Clinton was also tactless when he put forward ideas, creating friction at the top of the British command structure. Often, however, his proposals were better than the plans adopted by William Howe. (LOC, LC-USZ62-452)

RIGHT
Lieutenant-General Charles, Earl of Cornwallis (1738–1805). Cornwallis will forever be remembered for surrendering to Washington at Yorktown, but he credited the French artillery commander, d'Aboville, with his defeat, saying, "it was to you that I should have surrendered." (LOC, LC-USZ62-44927)

Howe was given command of the fleet that was to work in conjunction with his brother in 1776 and the two Howes were also granted limited powers as peace commissioners to negotiate an end to hostilities. Richard Howe's performance in the War of Independence is overshadowed by his brother's land-based activities, but he did well, never more so than when, after tendering his resignation, he remained in command long enough to fend off a large French fleet under d'Estaing in 1778.

Nicknamed "Black Dick" on account of his dark complexion, Howe's greatest success came after the War of Independence. He led the relief of Gibraltar in 1782 and was lauded for his actions as commander of naval forces in the Channel against the French in 1794 in the Glorious First of June.

Lieutenant-General Henry Clinton

One of the three major-generals sent to Boston in 1775, Clinton was with William Howe at Bunker Hill and was promoted to the local rank of lieutenant-general shortly afterwards. He is characterized as being a constant irritant to his commanding officers, pushing endless plans and stratagems on them with little tact, while retreating into overly cautious inactivity when in command himself. There is some truth in this, as poor relations with Howe as a subordinate and later Cornwallis as a superior bear out, but at least one of Clinton's suggestions was accepted with great effect—the flanking march at Long Island.

Also knighted in 1777, he returned to command the garrison of New York while Howe pursued Washington's army, but he was unable to intervene effectively on Burgoyne's behalf, a fact that he spent a good portion of his life trying to explain and excuse although he could hardly have been expected to do much more than he did.

Clinton became commander-in-chief on Howe's resignation, but the war had now become complicated by the arrival of French support. Taking the bulk of the blame for Cornwallis' defeat at Yorktown, Clinton worked hard to save his military career and ended it as Governor of Gibraltar in 1795.

Lieutenant-General Charles, Earl of Cornwallis

Having first served as an officer in the 1st Foot Guards, seeing action at the battle of Minden, Cornwallis sailed for America in January 1776 with the reinforcements for Clinton's Charleston campaign. After that misadventure he joined with Howe and took up position as his second in command at

Long Island, where he saw some of the fiercest fighting of the day at the Old Stone House.

It was Cornwallis' division that occupied Philadelphia in 1777 but he is (perhaps unfairly) remembered most for his surrender at Yorktown in 1781, effectively ending the war. It was the crowning misery of his dysfunctional relationship with Clinton, and his exploits in America were further tinged with sadness when his wife died during a visit home to Britain. He went on to better things in India, serving as governor-general from 1786 to 1794. As recognition for his fine service he was made 1st Marquis of Cornwallis in 1793.

Major-General Hugh, Earl Percy

Percy earned distinction as a lieutenant-colonel at the battles of Bergen and Minden, before entering politics and marrying Lord Bute's daughter. Popular, successful and well connected, he was aide-de-camp to George III by 1764. Despite disapproving of government policy toward the colonists he still offered his services, but, although his 5th Fusiliers were present at Bunker Hill, he was not—the result of either an illness or a disagreement with Howe, depending on whom you read. Promoted to major-general in September 1775, he commanded the rearguard of the flanking column at Long Island and was reportedly the first man to enter the fortifications at Fort Washington. Disagreements with Howe continued and, still unhappy with the war, he returned home in 1777, becoming Duke of Northumberland in 1786.

Major-General Hugh, Earl Percy (1742–1817). Percy was a talented soldier, but he was also known for the humane treatment of his men and his great generosity. Widows of his men killed at Bunker Hill were well provided for and he was a considerate landlord. (LOC, LC-USZ62-45225)

GERMAN

Lieutenant-General Leopold Philip von Heister

At the grand age of 69 von Heister was asked to lead the Hessian division by Landgrave Frederick II. Having first taken care to ensure his family would be taken care of should he die (and that all his debts would be written off immediately) he is reported to have declared: "Now your Serene Highness shall see what this old head and these bones can do."

Despite being a capable leader of men, and performing well at Long Island, von Heister's career was to end in bitter disappointment following the loss of the Hessian garrison at Trenton. A broken man, he returned home the following year and died "of grief and disappointment."

Lieutenant-General Wilhelm von Knyphausen (1716–1800). Von Knyphausen took over from von Heister as the commander-in-chief of German forces after the latter fell out with Howe and returned home. Those who saw him fight at Fort Washington professed amazement that he had not been killed or wounded. (LOC, LC-USZ62-52559)

Lieutenant-General Wilhelm von Knyphausen

Von Knyphausen's family had a history of serving alongside the British—his father had been colonel of a regiment that had fought with Marlborough. Though he joined the Prussian Army in 1735, it wasn't until 1775 that he was promoted to lieutenant-general and, like von Heister, he was advanced in years when he arrived in America with the second division of German mercenaries. Judging by accounts of his performance at Fort Washington, his first taste of action in America, von Knyphausen must have been a sprightly 60-year-old and he took over command of German forces when von Heister returned home in 1777. He only retired in 1782.

AMERICAN

General George Washington

A more iconic figure is hard to find than that of the leader of the American forces in the War of Independence. George Washington became the symbol

General George Washington (1732–99). For a long time an untouchable icon, modern historians tend to agree that Washington was an indifferent general early in his career—but he improved and, more importantly, was able to keep his army in the field, however small it occasionally became. (LOC, LC-USZ62-8272)

Major-General Nathaniel Greene (1742–86). Greene's absence at the battle of Long Island due to illness is often cited as a contributory factor to the defeat, and it certainly had an effect, but even he had thought fit to post only a five-man patrol at the otherwise open Jamaica Pass. (LOC, LC-USZ62-45507)

of American military strength and, although his abilities as a tactician have been justifiably questioned, his defining accomplishment was in somehow keeping an army in the field to oppose the British. That army may sometimes have dwindled to just a few thousand men, but it was always enough to keep the flame flickering. Washington also understood only too well the impact that even very minor victories could have on morale, public opinion and Britain's willingness to prolong the struggle, which is why his small-scale victories at Trenton and Princeton, coming after a string of British successes, were so crucial.

Washington served in the Virginia Militia in the French and Indian War and witnessed the fate of Major-General Edward Braddock at Monongahela in 1755. The life of a wealthy plantation owner beckoned, but he set it aside to take command of the Continental Army at Boston in 1775. He was frequently dismissive of his men's abilities, despaired of the short-term enlistments that constantly threatened to leave him with only a skeleton army and had to hold his force together in the face of British military superiority, a bungling and totally inadequate supply system, and brutally hard winters that were more of a risk than any number of redcoats.

Critically, as Washington's men learned, so did he, and he seems to have quickly realized that merely keeping an army in the field would eventually force the British to abandon a hugely expensive war. Independence won, he stepped down as commander-in-chief as the Continental Army was disbanded, but would go on to earn yet more distinction as his country's first president, in 1789.

Major-General Nathaniel Greene

Widely regarded as the best general on the American side, Greene turned his back on the peace-loving life of a Rhode Island Quaker family and had risen to brigadier-general by 1775. Originally in charge of the defenses at Long Island, he was taken ill with a fever and replaced by Israel Putnam just a week before the battle. Now a major-general, Greene subsequently saw his first action at Harlem Heights, which was a morale-boosting encounter for the Continentals, but he later made a serious error of judgment in trying to hold Fort Washington, resulting in one of the most severe reverses suffered by the Americans.

Greene improved with experience and did well at Monmouth, where he resisted an attack from Cornwallis that might have routed the Continentals. Further distinguished service followed at Newport, Rhode Island, on August 29, 1777, at the same time as he was performing well as quartermaster general. Disagreements with Congress dogged his career but Washington had great faith in his general and appointed him to command of the Southern Department in October 1780, where Greene put in his best work for the rebels. On March 15, 1781, he gave Cornwallis a mauling at Guildford Courthouse, helping to set the stage for Yorktown.

Financially ruined by the war, he took up residence at a plantation in Savannah, a gift of the people of Georgia for his service. He was just 44 when he died suddenly of sunstroke.

Major-General Charles Lee (1732–82)

Having served as an ensign in the British Army from 1744, advancing to lieutenant in the 44th Foot in 1751, Charles Lee saw action with Braddock, Horatio Gates, Washington and Thomas Gage in the French and Indian War.

As a colonel he distinguished himself under Burgoyne in Portugal in 1762 and, when his regiment was disbanded, he became a soldier of fortune, attaining the rank of major-general in the Polish Army in 1767. He therefore believed he had a strong claim to command the Continental Army when his allegiance switched to the Patriots. In the event he was second only to Washington, and although he performed well enough at Boston there was friction between the two men. Dispatched to attend to the fortification of New York in early 1776, he was later switched to command of the Southern Department and only returned to Washington in time for the engagement at White Plains.

Here his story takes a sad turn. Dawdling on his way to join forces with Washington in New Jersey, he was captured by a British patrol on December 13, 1776. While in captivity he offered the British advice on how to defeat the Americans, was considered for return to Britain to stand trial as a traitor and lost the novelty of a military background as his fellow generals in the Continental Army gained experience during his imprisonment. Finally exchanged in late 1777, he performed miserably at Monmouth, retreating when ordered to attack by Washington and prompting a ferocious and public exchange of opinions with the commander-in-chief on the battlefield. Following a court martial, a duel with Colonel John Laurens and, finally, dismissal from the Continental Army in 1780 after writing an incendiary letter to Congress, the man who once considered himself the ideal candidate to direct the struggle for independence withdrew in some disgrace to Philadelphia, where he died in 1782.

Major-General Charles Lee (1732–82). Lee, though a professional soldier, had a high opinion of the value of militia (in stark contrast to Washington), believing that they operated best as a "swarm of mosquitoes" to endlessly harass an enemy without presenting a solid target. (LOC, LC-USZ62-3617)

Major-General John Sullivan

Born in New Hampshire, Sullivan nailed his colors to the Patriotic mast early, leading a raid to seize weapons from Fort William and Mary in 1774. He served as a brigadier-general with Washington at Boston and was then ordered to join the American Army in Canada. Returning to Washington's side just in time to command the American positions at Long Island for four days, before being replaced by Israel Putnam, he was captured and quickly exchanged. Command of part of the attacking forces at Trenton and Princeton was followed by his expedition to subdue the Iroquois in northwestern New York. An army of 5,000 men was given to him for the task and his scorched-earth policy, though it made him a national hero for many years, has recently been seen as nothing more than attempted genocide. His last public duty was to serve as the governor of New Hampshire.

Major-General John Sullivan (1740–95). Sullivan acted as an envoy for the British while under captivity following Long Island, helping arrange a peace conference in September 1776 and earning the disdain of some of his fellow officers. (LOC, LC-USZ62-39567)

Major-General Israel Putnam

It is difficult to get a glimpse of the real Israel Putnam given the mass of legend that swirls around this colorful character. Even discounting the killing of a large wolf in her den, his story is remarkable. Nearly burnt at the stake by Indians in 1758, he was shipwrecked off Cuba, opened a tavern and married a wealthy widow. In 1779, at the age of 61, he reputedly galloped down a flight of rocky steps to escape capture by the British, a feat rendered no more likely by the building of a monument to it at the site.

His performance in the War of Independence was indifferent and he probably should never have risen above colonel. As a major-general he commanded the forces at Long Island, but the career of 'Old Put' slowly fizzled out after that. He retired from the army following a stroke in December 1779.

OPPOSING ARMIES

BRITISH AND GERMAN FORCES

With many popular histories and television documentaries proclaiming that Britain had a huge army at the start of the American War of Independence, it is enlightening to look at the figures that outline a total of around 48,000 men, spread thinly across the empire Britain had won in the Seven Years' War. The 8,500 or so men based in the colonies in 1775 was the largest body of men devoted to any single territory with the exception of England itself and Ireland. Far from being a militaristic state, Britain shared the same disdain for large standing armies as the rebellious colonists themselves and many victorious regiments of the Seven Years' War had been hastily disbanded as peace returned.

British troops were the victims of relentless and highly effective propaganda, with minor events like the "Boston Massacre" held up as examples of their cruelty and hatred of Americans. (LOC, LC-DIG-ppmsca-01657)

Clearly, this was not a sufficient number of men with which to restore order to colonies 3,000 miles away, but the effort involved in supplying Howe with an army worthy of the name almost defies belief. To make a modest start, existing forces could be shuffled around—five regiments of the Royal Hanoverian Army were sent to Gibraltar and Minorca, freeing the British regiments stationed there for service in America. Five of the Irish regiments were also assigned duties in America.

To find additional men would prove terribly difficult. Recruitment was not likely to be very productive. Secretary at War Viscount Barrington believed no more than 5,000 or 6,000 men could be found in this way. New recruits would preferably enter existing regiments—units started from scratch would inevitably take longer to reach battle readiness. The shattered remnants of the 18th and 59th Regiments, who suffered heavily at Bunker Hill, were absorbed into other regiments under Howe (a process known as "augmentation" that inevitably weakened the cohesion and fighting spirit of a regiment), while their officers and NCOs returned to Britain to hunt for recruits.

Lord North believed that new regiments were essential, but he met with resistance from the king, who disliked the expense involved and who also referred obliquely to "the different arrangements now just set in motion," which can't refer to anything else but the purchase of mercenary troops from a foreign power.

Part of the strained machinery that built William Howe's army to subdue America, Lord North was philosophically opposed to the war but nevertheless helped construct the largest expeditionary force Britain had ever assembled. (LOC, LC-USZ62-45299)

Recruitment was hindered by the actions of the East India Company, which ran its own army and recruited accordingly, effectively in competition with the army being put together for America. North hoped the East India Company might be willing to suspend recruitment, or at least reduce it, but the best offer to materialize was to limit recruitment to an area within 10 miles of London, obviously a very productive region.

Other possibilities included offers from men of private means to raise their own regiments. For the most part these offers were not taken up, but North was intrigued by an offer from a Mr Acland, an "independent man of fortune," whom North believed might bring a much-needed dash of glamour to the war. Comment is also made of an offer "in German which Lord North does not understand well enough to know even the name of the person from whom it comes." More welcome was the offer from Simon Fraser to raise a highland regiment. The 71st, Fraser's Highlanders, would number 2,000 men and would sail for the colonies with 1,000 fellow highlanders of the 42nd Regiment, the Black Watch.

Despite these gains, the proposed hired troops would obviously need to be of a substantial number. Initial hopes that Catherine the Great might supply 20,000 Russian troops were to come to nothing and by October 1775 efforts were focused on negotiations with the German states of Brunswick and Hesse-Cassell. With Howe wanting to strike by April of 1776, time was running out if sufficient men were to reach him. Finally, an agreement was made that would see 18,000 troops provided by Hesse-Cassell and Brunswick, and further good news came with the announcement that the Guards would be sending a composite force of over 1,000 officers and men.

A Hessian private from the Fusilier Regiment Erb Prinz of Hesse-Cassel, as depicted by Lieutenant Charles M. Lefferts. (1921.117, Collection of the New York Historical Society)

It was by now too late to get the men to Howe by April. Any consideration of the British forces that fought in 1776 must take account of the incredible logistical operation that was needed to get them to America. Ships had to be found to take 29 regiments, together with equipment, across the 3,000 miles of ocean between Europe and the rebellious colonies. More than 100 landing craft would be needed, along with around 300 heavy

wagons. Around 6,000 tons of shipping would be required just for the Irish regiments.

The creaky organization of the army was also a hindrance, and there was no official commander-in-chief of the British Army before Lord Amherst assumed the role in 1782. With no single powerful figure to orchestrate affairs it is perhaps surprising that Britain managed to get sizable numbers to Howe at all, but a force of 25,000 would eventually be at his disposal. Critical in the make-up of this army was the severe lack of mounted troops. The 17th Light Dragoons were Howe's only cavalry force and this would limit the ability to exploit a victory.

It must also be remembered that the struggle to subdue the colonists was being fought on two fronts. As well as Howe's army, Britain had to find sufficient men for Carleton in the north. The Americans had enjoyed success in Canada in 1775 and as the year closed they had possession of Montreal and were laying siege to Quebec. Furthermore, the capture of Fort Ticonderoga had given them access to the guns that were dragged southward to drive Howe out of Boston. The tide had turned at Quebec, but Carleton, the "Savior of Canada," received 8,000 reinforcements in May 1776. To find enough men for two fronts, both thousands of miles from home, had stretched the British logistical system to the limit.

AMERICAN FORCES

The army that built up in and around New York City was not the one that had performed so well around Boston, and, if Britain experienced problems in amassing an army to fight the war, they seem almost trivial compared to those that Washington had to deal with. The American commander-in-chief had to watch his army melt away as terms of enlistment expired at the end of 1775 and he was justifiably concerned that Howe's beleaguered regulars might break out and scatter the remains of his command. Less than 4,000 of the troops around Boston were willing to re-enlist and Washington was forced to call on emergency militia reinforcements. Even so, he had barely 10,000 men as 1776 opened.

The ragged men around Boston had become the Main Army, part of the Continental Army, following a vote in Congress on July 25. Congress was now attempting to raise a new army, but the term of enlistment would again be for a single year, which would put Washington in exactly the same situation in 12 months. It was entirely possible that the point would be moot by then and Washington lashed out angrily at what he saw as the "dirty, mercenary spirit" of the men who had left him at Boston.

Numbers were not the only problem. There was an almost total lack of military training to contend with as well. The painful fact was that Americans would have to learn their soldiering "on the job," and the lessons would be harsh. A key obstacle to overcome was the sense of rivalry between the colonies. One of the war's most celebrated diarists, Joseph Plumb Martin, wrote that he would rather serve alongside Indians than with men from Pennsylvania, whom he dismissed as "mostly foreigners." It was true that the fledgling Continental Army consisted of a broad spectrum of nationalities, and differences in social standing were no less dramatic. Freed slaves, gentlemen, farmers, paid substitutes, young glory seekers and a sprinkling of veterans would rub shoulders in the ranks.

There would be no effective training before Valley Forge in the winter of 1777, and the Continentals would for now have to settle for lessons offered by the British regulars on the field of battle. Nor was there any uniformity of dress. Congress had declared the uniform of the new army would consist of brown coats and all enlistees were entitled to one, but even the units who received brown coats soon wore them out and by late August Washington's army had a distinctly motley appearance. Notable exceptions were units including the 1st Delaware Regiment and Maryland's "Dandy Fifth," who would go into battle properly uniformed—for most it was a case of civilian clothes, or, at best, hunting shirts.

Equipment was similarly lacking in standardization, with a wide variety of weapons, including a few blunderbusses, joining British, Dutch, French and German muskets. Large numbers of French muskets, superior in some ways to the famed "Brown Bess" the British regulars carried, had started to arrive in 1776, but the problem was exacerbated by the tendency of fleeing soldiers to drop their weapons. An estimated 8,000 muskets were discarded in this way in 1776.

As John Milsop simply states, "Congress lacked the means to feed, pay, and equip its army." Regardless of this, the army existed, and around 28,500 men gathered around New York to oppose the British. Further indignity was heaped upon the men as sickness spread through New York and more than a quarter of Washington's army was incapacitated, giving him something less than 20,000 men who were fit for duty.

Less than half of this force was on the Continental establishment, with the remainder being state troops or militia. The soldiers came from eight of the 13 colonies, with Connecticut providing the largest group. Six Continental battalions, seven of "new levies" (raised in response to Congress's call for more troops) and 12 militia regiments from Connecticut were at Washington's disposal. Massachusetts delivered 11 Continental regiments and an artillery regiment under Colonel Henry Knox, with three militia regiments joining Washington in August, for a total of around 7,300 men. New York State itself furnished around 4,500 men, with two Continental regiments and nine militia battalions. The *city* of New York also delivered two battalions—the 1st New York Independent Battalion and the 2nd New York County Battalion, featuring such colorful company

The fine uniforms depicted in this 1779 painting are a far cry from the tattered array of uniforms, hunting shirts and civilian dress in which Washington's men took the field in 1776. (LOC, LC-USZ62-12383)

The action at Lexington and Concord had shown what untrained militia could do. The British lost 300 killed, wounded and missing as a cloud of militia swarmed about them. The Americans then closed in on the beleaguered British forces at Boston and commenced the siege that set the stage for Bunker Hill. (Domenick D'Andrea)

names as the "Prussian Blues," the "Hearts of Oak," the "Sportsmen," the "Hussars" and the "Scotsmen."

Pennsylvania's representation at New York comprised three Continental battalions and five of militia, giving a total of over 3,000 men. New Jersey had 1,500 men with Washington, in the form of five battalions of new levies, while Maryland delivered around 900 men—one regiment (the "Dandy Fifth") and four independent companies.

Rhode Island was represented by two Continental battalions, totaling around 800 men (Rhode Island would raise a further regiment that reached Washington in September, too late to take part in the battle of Long Island). Finally, Delaware contributed a single regiment of Continentals, but, numbering around 750, it was the largest in Washington's army. It is also worth noting that the small contingents from Maryland and Delaware would punch above their weight on Long Island.

The rebels too had to contend with a division of forces. The campaign in Canada demanded its share of troops, including two Continental regiments from New York, three from New Jersey and four from Pennsylvania.

Washington was also almost totally devoid of cavalry—indeed, he had turned down the offer of three cavalry regiments from Connecticut in June. This force, numbering around 400, could have performed very valuable work in patrolling the outlying American defenses, but Washington believed the difficulty in feeding the horses would outweigh their usefulness (a curious belief given the time of the year and the abundance of suitable fodder on Long Island). He asked the men to serve as foot soldiers, with their horses sent to Westchester to serve as remounts for officers or work animals. The Connecticut cavalrymen turned this offer down. Developments on Long Island would make this deficiency in cavalry telling. The only sizable body of mounted troops Washington did control was that of the Long Island Militia, under Nathaniel Woodhull, and they were employed exclusively in rounding up and driving livestock to keep it from falling into British hands.

ORDERS OF BATTLE – THE BATTLE OF LONG ISLAND, AUGUST 27, 1776

BRITISH FORCES

Overall command: General William Howe

CLINTON'S DIVISION – LIEUTENANT-GENERAL SIR HENRY CLINTON

1st Battalion Light Infantry
2nd Battalion Light Infantry
3rd Battalion Light Infantry

CLEVELAND'S DIVISION – BRIGADIER-GENERAL SAMUEL CLEVELAND

1st Artillery Brigade
2nd Artillery Brigade
3rd Artillery Brigade

1st Brigade – Major-General James Robertson
    4th Regiment of Foot
    15th Regiment of Foot
    27th Regiment of Foot
    45th Regiment of Foot

2nd Brigade – Major-General Robert Pigot
    5th Regiment of Foot
    28th Regiment of Foot
    35th Regiment of Foot
    49th Regiment of Foot

5th Brigade – Brigadier-General Francis Smith
    22nd Regiment of Foot
    43rd Regiment of Foot

54th Regiment of Foot
63rd Regiment of Foot

6th Brigade – Major-General James Agnew
    23rd Regiment of Foot
    44th Regiment of Foot
    57th Regiment of Foot
    64th Regiment of Foot

Guards – Major-General Edward Mathew
    1st Battalion Guards
    2nd Battalion Guards

Cavalry – Major-General George Preston
    17th Light Dragoons

PERCY'S DIVISION – LIEUTENANT-GENERAL HUGH EARL PERCY

3rd Brigade – Major-General Valentine Jones
    10th Regiment of Foot
    37th Regiment of Foot
    38th Regiment of Foot
    52nd Regiment of Foot

4th Brigade – Major-General James Grant
    17th Regiment of Foot
    40th Regiment of Foot
    46th Regiment of Foot
    55th Regiment of Foot

Fraser's Highlanders – Brigadier-General William Erskine
    1st Battalion 71st, Fraser's Highlanders
    2nd Battalion 71st, Fraser's Highlanders
    3rd Battalion 71st, Fraser's Highlanders

Reserves – Lieutenant-General Charles Earl Cornwallis
  1st Battalion Grenadiers
  2nd Battalion Grenadiers
  3rd Battalion Grenadiers
  4th Battalion Grenadiers
  33rd Regiment of Foot
  42nd Regiment of Foot

HESSIAN DIVISION – LIEUTENANT-GENERAL LEOPOLD PHILIP VON HEISTER

Baron Wilhelm von Knyphausen, second in command (arrived after the battle of Long Island)
Mirbach's Brigade – Major-General von Mirbach
  Fusilier Regiment von Knyphausen
  Fusilier Regiment von Lossberg
  Grenadier Regiment von Rall

Stirn's Brigade – Major-General J. D. von Stirn
  Musketeer Regiment von Donop
  Musketeer Regiment von Mirbach
  Fusilier Regiment Erb Prinz (Hereditary Prince)

Donop's Brigade – Colonel Count Carl von Donop
  Grenadier Battalion von Linsing
  Grenadier Battalion von Block
  Grenadier Battalion von Minegrode
  Jäger Corps

Note:
In addition to these troops, a further brigade of Hessians remained at Staten Island during the battle of Long Island. This was Lossberg's Brigade and was led by Colonel von Lossberg. The constituent regiments were the Regiments von Ditfurth and von Trumbach.

AMERICAN ARMY
Overall command: General George Washington
Commander of Artillery: Colonel Henry Knox
Commanding in Brooklyn: Major-General Israel Putnam

Note:
Following is a complete list of units that were with Washington in and around New York. Those marked * were present on Long Island on August 22, the day of the British landings. Those marked ** were transferred to Long Island before the battle commenced on August 27. Those marked *** were transferred to Long Island after the battle had commenced.

PUTNAM'S DIVISION – MAJOR-GENERAL ISRAEL PUTNAM
Aide-de-camp Major Aaron Burr

Clinton's Brigade – Brigadier-General James Clinton (absent during the summer and commanded by Colonel Read and Colonel Glover)
Brigade Major David Henly
  3rd Cont. (Mass.), Colonel Joseph Read
  13th Cont. (Mass.), Colonel Ebenezer Learned
  23rd Cont. (Mass.), Colonel John Bailey
  26th Cont. (Mass.), Colonel Loammi Baldwin

Scott's Brigade – Brigadier-General John Morin Scott
Brigade Major Nicholas Fish
  1st New York Independent Battalion, Colonel John Lasher**
  2nd New York County Battalion, Colonel William Malcolm***
  New York Militia Regiment, Colonel Samuel Drake**
  New York Militia Regiment, Colonel Cornelius Humphrey***

Fellows' Brigade – Brigadier-General John Fellows
Brigade Major Mark Hopkins
  Worcester County (Mass.) Militia, Colonel Jonathan Holman
  Plymouth and Bristol County (Mass.), Colonel Simeon Cary
  Berkshire County (Mass.) Militia, Colonel Jonathan Smith
  14th Cont. (Mass.) "The Marblehead Regiment," Colonel John Glover***

HEATH'S DIVISION – MAJOR-GENERAL WILLIAM HEATH
Aides-de-camp Major Thomas Henly, Major Israel Keith
Mifflin's Brigade – Brigadier-General Thomas Mifflin

Brigade Major Jonathan Mifflin
  3rd Pennsylvania Battalion, Colonel Robert Magaw***
  5th Pennsylvania Battalion, Colonel John Shee***
  16th Cont. (Mass.) , Colonel Israel Hutchinson
  27th Cont. (Mass.) , Colonel Paul Dudley Sargent
  Ward's (Conn.) Battalion, Colonel Andrew Ward

Clinton's Brigade – Brigadier-General George Clinton
Brigade Major Albert Pawling
  New York Militia Regiment, Colonel Isaac Nichol
  New York Militia Regiment, Colonel Thomas Thomas
  New York Militia Regiment, Colonel James Swartwout
  New York Militia Regiment, Colonel Levi Paulding
  New York Militia Regiment, Colonel Morris Graham

SPENCER'S DIVISION –
MAJOR-GENERAL JOSEPH SPENCER

Aides-de-camp William Peck, Major Charles Whiting

Parsons' Brigade – Brigadier-General Samuel Holden
Parsons
Brigade Major Thomas Dyer
 10th Cont. (Conn.), Colonel Jedediah Huntington
 (Lieutenant-Colonel Joel Clark)**
 17th Cont. (Conn.), Colonel Samuel Wyllys**
 20th Cont. (Conn.), Colonel John Durkee
 21st Cont. (Mass.), Colonel John Tyler
 22nd Cont. (Conn.), Colonel Jonathan Ward**

Wadsworth's Brigade – Brigadier-General James Wadsworth
Brigade Major Jon Palsgrave Wyllys
 Connecticut Levies, Colonel Gold Selleck Silliman**
 Connecticut Levies, Colonel Fisher Gay
 Connecticut Levies, Colonel Comfort Sage***
 Connecticut Levies, Colonel Samuel Selden***
 Connecticut Levies, Colonel William Douglas***
 Connecticut Levies, Colonel John Chester**
 Connecticut Levies, Colonel Phillip Burr Bradley

SULLIVAN'S DIVISION –
MAJOR-GENERAL JOHN SULLIVAN

Aides-de-camp Major Alexander Scammell, Major Lewis
Morris, Jr

Stirling's Brigade – Brigadier-General William Alexander,
Lord Stirling
Brigade Major W. S. Livingston
 5th Maryland Regiment, Colonel William Smallwood**
 1st Delaware Regiment, Colonel John Haslet**
 Pennsylvania Rifle Regiment, Colonel Samuel Miles**
 Pennsylvania Musketeers, Colonel Samuel Jon Atlee**
 Pennsylvania Militia Regiment, Lieutenant-Colonel
 Nicholas Lutz**
 Pennsylvania Militia Regiment, Lieutenant-Colonel Peter
 Kachlein**
 Lancaster County (Pennsylvania) Militia Battalion, Major
 William Hay**

McDougall's Brigade – Brigadier-General Alexander
McDougall
Brigade Major Richard Platt
 1st New York Regiment, late McDougall's
 3rd New York Regiment, Colonel Rudolph Ritzema
 19th Cont. (Conn.), Colonel Charles Webb***
 Artificers, Colonel Jonathan Brewer

GREENE'S DIVISION –
MAJOR-GENERAL NATHANIEL GREENE

Aides-de-camp Major William Blodgett, Major William S.
Livingston
Nixon's Brigade – Brigadier-General John Nixon
Brigade Major Daniel Box
 1st Cont. (Penn.), Colonel Edward Hand*
 9th Cont. (RI), Colonel James Mitchell Varnum*
 11th Cont. (RI), Colonel Daniel Hitchcock*
 4th Colonial Infantry (Mass. Battalion), Lieutenant-
 Colonel Thomas Nixon
 7th Colonial Infantry (Mass. Battalion), Colonel William
 Prescott
 12th Cont. (Mass.), Colonel Moses Little*

Heard's Brigade – Brigadier General Nathaniel Heard
Brigade Major Peter Gordon
 New Jersey (New Levies), Colonel David Forman*
 New Jersey (New Levies), Colonel Phillip Johnston*
 New Jersey (New Levies), Colonel Ephraim Martin*
 New Jersey (New Levies), Colonel Silas Newcomb*
 New Jersey Militia Regiment, Colonel Phillip Van
 Cortlandt*

Connecticut Militia – Brigadier-General Oliver Wolcott
 Connecticut Militia Regiment, Colonel Thompson
 Connecticut Militia Regiment, Colonel Hinman
 Connecticut Militia Regiment, Colonel Pettibone
 Connecticut Militia Regiment, Colonel Cooke
 Connecticut Militia Regiment, Colonel Talcott
 Connecticut Militia Regiment, Colonel Chapman
 Connecticut Militia Regiment, Colonel Baldwin
 Connecticut Militia Regiment, Lieutenant-Colonel Mead
 Connecticut Militia Regiment, Lieutenant-Colonel Lewis
 Connecticut Militia Regiment, Lieutenant-Colonel Pitkin
 Connecticut Militia Regiment, Major Strong
 Connecticut Militia Regiment, Major Newberry

Long Island Militia – Brigadier-General Nathaniel Woodhull
 Suffolk County (NY) Militia, Colonel Josiah Smith
 King's and Queen's County (NY) Militia, Colonel
 Jeronimus Remsen

Artillery
Massachusetts, Colonel Henry Knox

OPPOSING PLANS

BRITISH PLANS

Even while British forces had been bottled up at Boston, key figures had been considering New York as a more suitable starting point for an offensive campaign in 1776. The position of the colony, dividing New England from the south, made it strategically important. New England was seen as the driving force behind the revolution, while the southern states provided the supplies needed to maintain resistance against the British. This no doubt oversimplified matters, but the convenient location of the Hudson River, neatly dividing the colonies in two, made it seem possible to cut off the militant New Englanders from their supply base.

In fact, so seductive was this strategy that no other appears to have been seriously proposed, save for that of the Secretary at War, Viscount Barrington, who favored a naval blockade and only limited land-based operations. The Hudson strategy also had the benefit of allowing Britain to concentrate on one area with the hope of attaining complete success. Anyone with a grasp of military reality would know that actually conquering all 13 colonies was an impossibility with the limited resources at hand. The apparent possibility of forcing the colonists to give up their struggle by such a simple method as controlling a river must have been irresistible.

New York had originally been New Amsterdam. A British army under the Duke of York, younger brother of Charles II, had taken it in a bloodless campaign that in many ways was startlingly similar to that of 1776—a landing at Gravesend Bay took place on August 26, 1664, while British troops occupied what was now "New York" on September 8. (LOC, LC-USZ62-46068)

Howe's army would be the main force in the strategy. Having established a base at New York he would move up the Hudson to link up with a smaller army under Carleton moving down it. Having secured the length of the Hudson the British could then launch expeditions against New England. The only major obstacle, it appeared, was Washington's Main Army. With a large enemy army in the field the British would never be able to maintain control of the Hudson—isolated garrisons would be easily overwhelmed by a sizable force and the aim of cutting off New England from the other colonies would be unattainable. For the strategy to succeed, the Main Army needed to be crippled or, better yet, destroyed entirely.

The replacement of Dartmouth with Germain as Colonial Secretary was a factor in the decision to wage an aggressive campaign against the Americans. Germain shared the opinion of many that "one decisive blow on land is absolutely necessary." He also believed it might be *all* that was necessary, a comforting notion considering his doubts about the possibility of actually conquering the entire country. "As there is not common sense in protracting a war of this sort," he commented, "I should be for exerting the utmost force of this kingdom to finish the rebellion in one campaign."

Previously known as Lord George Sackville, Germain had been court-martialed for his slowness to respond to an order at the battle of Minden and had been declared "unfit to serve his majesty in any military capacity whatever." (LOC, LC-USZ62-45273)

The king had no control over the finer details of military operations in America, but he was hawkish in the extreme and felt the colonists needed to be taught a sharp lesson by Howe's army. (LOC, LC-USZ62-7819)

LEFT
"Yankee Doodle 1776"— an effective depiction by Archibald M. Willard of the often disheveled but stubborn men of all ages who fought in the war for independence. (LOC, LC-USZC4-694)

This view of New York, emphasizing as it does the waterways enveloping the city, is a good indication of why the British felt it would make a fine starting point to restoring order in the colonies. (LOC, LC-USZ62-46050)

Perversely, the difficulties with which Howe had extricated his army from Boston now worked in his favor. Unable to move directly to New York because of the disorganization of his evacuation of Boston, the loss of supplies and the limited number of transports, he had been forced to go to Halifax, giving Washington the chance to make perhaps his most serious mistake of the war—the decision to defend New York.

British military preparations were given an added twist by the fact that the Howe brothers were also authorized to act as peace commissioners. This would put them in the awkward position of attacking rebel forces in the field at the same time as attempting reconciliation and the duties would probably have been better undertaken by separate parties. The affection the Howes both felt for the colonists is also an important factor to consider. Would William Howe be willing to destroy Washington's army if he got the chance? His performance around New York would make that a very interesting question indeed.

AMERICAN PLANS

Washington's army, as it stood in 1776, was not capable of defending New York, but there was immense political pressure not simply to give the city up. Certainly the uncontested loss of a major city would have been a severe blow to the morale of the soldiers under Washington. Conceding the inability to oppose the British military juggernaut was not the way to start a campaign.

Washington decided to stand, therefore, and was immediately faced with the near impossibility of the situation. British naval supremacy meant that a good deal of the defensive effort had to be expended on limiting the range of the Royal Navy's warships. Situated on the tip of Manhattan (or York) Island, the city could be bypassed by ships on both the North (Hudson) and East rivers. To cut off the Hudson, Fort Washington was constructed midway along Manhattan on the commanding heights of Mount Washington and further batteries were placed on Paulus Hook in New Jersey.

Emplacements in New York City itself protected the East River, but these themselves were vulnerable to any guns placed on the Brooklyn Heights on Long Island. Washington was forced to build fortifications there as well to prevent the British from simply occupying the high ground and compelling the evacuation of New York. The Main Army, with no naval support, would therefore be split over two islands in the face of a major maritime power and a superior army.

Work at Brooklyn commenced in February 1776, under plans drawn up by Charles Lee, but Lee himself had ventured the opinion that New York could not be held. He hoped merely to turn it into "an advantageous field of battle." When Lee was sent south to Charleston Brigadier-General William

A rather fanciful depiction of a "Patriot of 1776 defending his homestead." The patriot in question has laid one dragoon low and is setting about another. (LOC, LC-USZ62-20453)

Alexander, who claimed the title of Lord Stirling, took up the work. Lee's plans for three redoubts and entrenchments to protect the Brooklyn Heights from attack from the East River were changed and a single fort was constructed instead, Fort Stirling. Interestingly, no efforts had yet been made to protect these works from an attack from the interior of Long Island. It was not until July that Colonel Rufus Putnam initiated works to remedy this situation. A string of forts and redoubts was stretched across the Brooklyn Peninsula, anchored at both sides by marshland and inviting a costly frontal assault. Two more forts (Defiance and Cobble Hill) completed the rebel defenses at Brooklyn.

Washington based his strategy on the hope that the British would be unimaginative in their assault. He had constructed defensive works at Brooklyn and throughout Manhattan, hoping to exact heavy losses at each point. A ridge of high ground running across Long Island, the Gowanus Heights, was later adopted as a forward defensive line. Initially only an extra zone of resistance, Washington came to view this as the best chance of stopping the British. The slope was gentle on the defending side, steep and heavily wooded on the other, and it was easily passable only at a small number of places. Troops were placed at each pass behind felled trees and it was hoped that the British would get no farther.

Under the direction of Israel Putnam the Americans also seized and fortified Governors Island and hulks were sunk between it and the battery at the tip of Manhattan to further impede British shipping. It is impossible not to wonder why further defensive works were not constructed to guard the narrow stretch of water between Staten Island and Long Island, but the fact is that the Americans had limited resources and manpower. They had done what they could but Washington, quite rightly, had a sense of foreboding. "We expect a very bloody summer …" he wrote his brother on May 31, "and I am sorry to say that we are not, either in men or arms, prepared for it."

THE BATTLE OF LONG ISLAND

Two weeks after leaving Halifax, William Howe's ship, the *Greyhound*, was sighted off Long Island. Over the next few days the remainder of his fleet arrived, but Howe's original intention, to land at Gravesend Bay on Long Island, was revised when he discovered the state of affairs on Long Island. Intelligence reports informed Howe that the rebels "are numerous and very advantageously posted with strong entrenchments both upon Long Island and that of New York, with more than 100 cannon for the defence of the town towards the sea, and to obstruct the passage of the fleet up the North [Hudson] River." The defensive works at Brooklyn also gave Howe pause, and he decided to make his initial landing at Staten Island.

There was now no doubt in Howe's mind that he needed reinforcements before taking the offensive. "I propose waiting here for the English Fleet, or for the arrival of Lieut. General Clinton, in readiness to proceed, ..." he wrote to Germain. This seems to imply that he did not feel he needed to await *all* of his reinforcements, only a part of them. The letter was written on July 7, 1776. Howe would not have known that three days earlier the war had taken on a different tone with the issuing of the Declaration of Independence.

The length of time it took for letters to reach London meant that it was six weeks before Germain prepared his reply, in which he carefully stated that he believed Howe was entirely correct in waiting for "one of the expected reinforcements." Germain was probably beginning to lose patience with the

A view of the city of New York as seen from Long Island. This is where British efforts to defeat the rebel army would begin, but delays in starting the campaign had given the Americans time to fortify both islands. (LOC, LC-USZ62-20492)

The British build-up, 1776

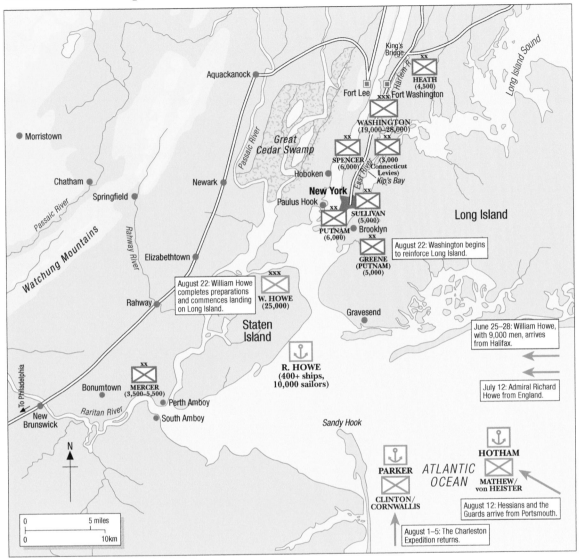

delays and would no doubt have been alarmed to know that, as he wrote his reply to Howe on August 22, the general had still not taken New York.

Inevitably in such a huge operation, not all was going smoothly. A portion of Fraser's Highlanders had mistakenly sailed for Boston and had been captured by American privateers. Howe also complained of a lack of camp equipment, which might seem like an excuse for inactivity but was important in 18th-century warfare to ensure the health of the troops in the field. Still, Howe's reluctance to move is puzzling. Did he overestimate American strength, or was he still mindful of his experience at Bunker Hill? Whatever the reason, he was now set on receiving all of his reinforcements before moving.

On July 12 Admiral Howe's flagship, the *Eagle*, appeared, but extra soldiers did not start to appear until August 1, when Clinton's rather battered expedition returned from Charleston. Finally, on August 12, the arrival of the Hessians and Guards boosted Howe's total strength to around 25,000. The British fleet numbered around 400, with some 10,000 sailors, and it

Looking from the battery out to Governors Island in a photograph from around 1911. In 1776 hulks were sunk between Manhattan and Governors Island in an attempt to prevent British warships from moving freely. (LOC, LC-USZ62-135430)

BELOW, RIGHT
The tearing down of the statue of George III, and its subsequent melting down for musket balls, caused one excited observer to hope that Britain's soldiers might soon have "molten majesty" fired upon them. (LOC, LC-USZ62-22023)

made for a spectacular sight: "I thought all London was afloat," commented one observer. Howe was now prepared to move and wrote to Germain once more on August 15, stating "no time will be lost in proceeding upon the operations of the campaign."

While some have viewed Howe's slowness as a mistake, it actually increased the chances of securing a major victory at New York. As numbers grew on both sides Washington was able to commit more troops to Long Island, which would be a very difficult place to evacuate if the British got the upper hand. Howe's delays therefore served mainly to bring a larger number of rebel soldiers within his reach.

Washington was in an agony of indecision, unsure of where the first blow would land. Howe might bypass Long Island totally and land on Manhattan; he might also go still further and pen the entire Main Army in by seizing Kingsbridge and Freebridge, the two land routes off Manhattan. Washington's troop dispositions betrayed this indecision. The divisions of Putnam, Sullivan and Spencer, along with the Connecticut Militia, were spread around the city of New York. Jonathan Mifflin's Brigade was at Fort

Washington and George Clinton's Brigade was to be found at Kingsbridge. Only two brigades (and the Long Island Militia) were currently based on Long Island—John Nixon's and Nathaniel Heard's Brigades of Nathaniel Greene's Division, totaling just over 3,000 men. (Two regiments, Nixon's and Prescott's Massachusetts units of Nixon's Brigade, were posted at Governors Island.)

These 3,000 or so men were extremely vulnerable to any sizable force attacking from the interior of the island and were also at risk of being cut off if the British moved on New York City, but Howe's decision to start at Long Island had as much to do with the fact that it was rich in crops and livestock. Taking Long Island may have lacked the dash of a maneuver to get behind Washington, but it promised a ready source of supplies for his army. American efforts to deny these supplies to Howe (Woodhull, with the 500 Long Island Militia, was tasked with driving cattle out of the reach of the British and with burning crops) were only partly successful and nothing like a scorched-earth policy was pursued.

An attempt to prevent the British fleet from entering the Lower and Upper Bays may have changed the course of the confrontation. Colonel William Douglas, at 34 a veteran of the French and Indian War, had realized that the narrow passageways between Sandy Hook and Coney Island, and the Narrows between Staten Island and Long Island itself, would be good places to block the entry of British shipping, but the realization came too late to be acted upon. When Howe's fleet moved through the Narrows on July 2 they would have been vulnerable to guns on either side, but only a battery of 9-pdrs was in place to offer a token of resistance and a few defiant rebels fired muskets.

On July 9 Washington's men were given a boost to morale with the reading of the Declaration of Independence. Fired with a patriotic zeal, civilians and soldiers alike tore down the statue of George III at Bowling Green. A symbolic act of defiance, this also had a practical angle as the 4,000lb of lead could be melted down to make musket balls. Work was continuing at the fortifications on Manhattan and Long Island, but a simple demonstration of their ineffectiveness came on July 12, when two British ships, the *Phoenix* and the *Rose*, sailed up the North River in defiance of the

The attack by fireships on the *Phoenix* and the *Rose* did not damage the two main vessels, but a smaller bomb ketch was sunk. (LOC, LC-USZ62-45594)

guns at Fort Washington, which was still under construction at the time. The ships fired several shots into the city, provoking panic and the flaw in the American plan was clear. If they could not stop the Royal Navy from sailing at will up the Hudson, then New York was untenable.

Stung by this demonstration, the Americans struck back by attempting to burn the two British vessels with fireships on August 16, and even though the attempt proved unsuccessful it does seem to have caused genuine concern. The *Phoenix* and the *Rose* headed back down the Hudson on August 18 in time to prove that further American efforts at hindering their passage—a string of sunken hulks stretched across the width of the river—were still insufficient to cause anything other than a mild inconvenience. Washington ordered a further fort to be built opposite Fort Washington, on the Jersey side. Fort Constitution (which later became known as Fort Lee) would be able to operate in conjunction with Fort Washington to catch British ships in a crossfire if they attempted to sail up the Hudson again.

"The Conference between the Brothers HOW to get rich"—William and Richard Howe are portrayed as plotting to prolong the war to increase their personal wealth, with encouragement from the devil himself. (LOC, LC-USZ62-41467)

While these tentative exchanges played out, efforts were made to find a peaceful resolution to the crisis. Lord Howe had found his powers as a peace commissioner seriously undermined by the Declaration of Independence—he had no authority to negotiate with an independent state, only to offer pardons to those who returned to an allegiance to the king—but he made an effort anyway. It almost immediately foundered on the point of Washington's title. Unwilling to accept his position as general in a foreign army, Howe merely addressed him as "George Washington Esq." in his first written communication. The aides sent to meet with Howe's envoy refused to accept this term of address. A later letter addressed to "George Washington, Esq. and etc. etc." was also deemed insufficient.

A solution was found by making a verbal, rather than written request for "His Excellency General Washington" to meet with Lieutenant-Colonel James Paterson, the adjutant general of the British Army. The meeting produced nothing, however, as Washington insisted that the former colonists had no need of pardons, having done nothing wrong. The time for negotiation had passed and only military force might now change the minds of the rebels.

OPENING MOVES

On the night of August 21 a severe thunderstorm broke over New York. Several Americans were struck by lightning and killed and some saw this as a bad omen. For several days Howe had been loading his men back onto transport ships. Their pleasant stay on Staten Island, no doubt hugely welcome after the weeks of miserable captivity during the journey from Britain, had restored them to fighting fitness and this time the voyage by water would be a short one. On August 22 the first troops were ferried over to Long Island, Clinton and Cornwallis commanding the spearhead—4,000 men landing at Denyse's Ferry—with 5,000 more quickly following to land at Gravesend Bay. The 200–300 men of Colonel Edward Hand's 1st Pennsylvania Continentals could only sound the warning and withdraw. Unmolested, the British landed a total of around 15,000 men and 40 cannons.

The flotilla moved across the Narrows in ten divisions; and following it came transports with eleven thousand more troops and forty pieces of artillery. All were debarked before noon. These fifteen thousand men took possession of the roads, and occupied the Dutch villages of Utrecht, Gravesend, and Flat-

Passage of the Troops to Long Island.

The transfer of British troops to Long Island was a well-coordinated affair that might have been made less straightforward had the Americans defended the shoreline of Long Island. (Picture Collection, The Branch Libraries, The New York Public Library, Astor, Lenox and Tilden Foundations)

Washington was still uncertain that the British intended to attack on Long Island. Intelligence reports suggested only around 9,000 troops had landed and further estimated the total size of the British Army at as much as 35,000 men. If that was the case Howe could certainly mount a major assault elsewhere and the troops on Long Island could be a diversion. Cautiously, Washington ordered a reinforcement of just six regiments to cross over to Brooklyn: the Pennsylvania Rifle Regiment and Pennsylvania Musketeers under Samuel Miles and Samuel John Atlee, respectively, from Lord Stirling's Brigade; two regiments of Connecticut levies under Gold Selleck Silliman and John Chester of James Wadsworth's Brigade; and the 1st New York Independent Battalion and a regiment of New York Militia under John Lasher and Samuel Drake, respectively, both of Scott's Brigade. This reinforcement totaled around 1,800 men, bringing total strength on Long Island, including Woodhull's Militia, to around 5,400.

American preparations were being hampered by the absence of Nathaniel Greene, taken ill at a most inopportune moment. On August 20 Washington replaced him with John Sullivan, but while the commander-in-chief had doubts about Sullivan's ability, it was the replacement commander on Long Island who saw the potential of the Gowanus Heights and ordered them to be defended. Each route through the Heights—the Shore (or Narrows) Road and Martense Lane, Flatbush Pass and Bedford Pass—would be defended by between 500 and 1,000 men. Given the steep slope of the Gowanus Heights and the thick woodland across it, it was believed that such numbers would be sufficient to hold up a much larger attacking force. Even should the passes fall, the inflicting of large numbers of casualties might force the British to accept only a pyrrhic victory.

Elsewhere, the five forts and redoubts that strung across the neck of the Brooklyn Peninsula were completed, although opinion is divided on how formidable an obstacle they presented. To a distance of around 100 yards in front of the entrenchments, trees had been cut down to deny cover to an assaulting force. A ditch was constructed in front of the lines and the trees that had been felled to create the killing ground were piled in front of the trenches to form an abatis. A total of 28 landward-facing cannons, mostly 18-pdrs, were placed in the forts and redoubts that dotted Brooklyn, with 35 more facing the sea, ranging in size from 12- to 32-pdrs.

Despite the disparity in numbers it was possible that the Americans might administer a severe setback to British hopes if one crucial element fell the Americans' way—Howe's army needed to mount a simple, frontal assault on the American defenses for them to operate as designed. In this respect, the error made by the Americans in neglecting to defend a fourth possible route through the Gowanus Heights was unforgivable.

The major road running through the string of fortifications at Brooklyn led to Jamaica. It was envisioned that the British might advance down this road and be caught in an indentation in the lines, subject to fire from different angles. The road to Jamaica ran through the Gowanus Heights at the Jamaica Pass and although this was a considerable distance from the American defenses it was an obvious route for the British to take. Unless the Americans assumed that the British would undertake no reconnaissance before attacking there seems no reason to have left the pass undefended.

The subject would become the cause of intense debate—because the British *did* undertake a reconnaissance and they *did* discover that the pass was unguarded. It appears that Henry Clinton was the man who suggested a flanking march to Howe. Having grown up on Long Island his words probably carried extra weight even though Howe found Clinton's constant advice to be tiresome. In this instance there was simply no way to ignore the fact that a flanking march could entirely undermine the Americans' advanced line, bypassing the defenses at each of the other passes and allowing the British to move on to the next line for a very small price. Having been resigned to a potentially costly frontal assault on the passes, something he was determined to avoid if at all possible, Howe must have been relieved to have an alternative handed to him.

Changes in the command structure of the Americans on Long Island cannot have helped the situation. Sullivan, who had only taken command on August 20, was in turned replaced as overall commander of forces in the area by Israel Putnam on August 24. Putnam did not know Long Island and apparently made little effort to learn anything about it.

The British plan was extremely simple, as most successful plans are. Diversionary attacks would be made at the right and centre of the American line, at the Shore Road–Martense Lane Pass and the Flatbush Pass. Major-General James Grant would command a force of around 3,000 men (with the addition of around 2,000 marines) at the former, while the Hessian Division, boosted by the arrival of two further brigades on August 25 and under Lieutenant-General Leopold Philip von Heister, would operate in the centre alongside the 42nd Regiment. The main force, some 10,000 strong and led by Howe himself, would undertake a lengthy march under cover of darkness to the Jamaica Pass. This force would include the light infantry under Clinton in the vanguard, with the 17th Light Dragoons acting as a screen. Silence was of paramount importance and the British allowed themselves 12 hours to make the march, which would cover around five miles to the Jamaica Pass and three more to the village of Bedford, behind the American lines at the Gowanus Heights. Here, at 0900hrs on August 27, signal shots would be fired and the attack on all three sections of the American line would begin in earnest.

Simple it may have been, but the march would still be a commendable feat if carried out without a hitch. The entire column would be two miles or more in length and would inevitably make noise whatever measures were taken to minimize it. Although trees in the way could be sawn down rather than chopped and wheels could be muffled, the danger of discovery remained very real.

American forces on Long Island were increased still further on August 24, when Washington ordered over more reinforcements: the 10th, 17th and 22nd Continentals (Connecticut) of Samuel Holden Parsons' Brigade, under

Israel Putnam was in charge on Long Island as British forces built up, but quick-fire changes from Greene (who was ill), to Sullivan (who was replaced) to Putnam must have been a distraction when the Americans least needed one. (LOC, LC-USZ62-5666)

The 17th Light Dragoons were Howe's only mounted troops, with a sinister skull and crossbones on their helmets and the motto "Death or Glory." They fulfilled a valuable scouting and screening role prior to and during the battle of Long Island. (Lieutenant Charles M. Lefferts: 1920.149, Collection of the New York Historical Society)

Jedediah Huntington, Samuel Wyllys and John Tyler, respectively; and two Pennsylvania Militia units under Nicholas Lutz and Major Hay. August 24 was the date on which Lord Stirling crossed to Brooklyn and it also saw Washington's decision to replace Sullivan as overall commander on Long Island. Washington was apparently dissatisfied with Sullivan's performance in the few days he had been in command, particularly disapproving of the sometimes lively skirmishing instigated by American forces. Certainly Washington's orders to Putnam were explicit: he was to remain on the defensive. The least experienced soldiers were to man the Brooklyn lines, while the best troops were to be placed along the Gowanus Heights, which they were to hold "at all hazards."

On the morning of August 26 Washington himself toured the Brooklyn defenses and ordered that a unit of 500 men under Samuel Miles should patrol the area between the Bedford and Jamaica passes. It was a large area for 500 men to cover and, far from solidifying the left flank, it left it in jeopardy. The action also removed any possibility of Washington claiming not to know about the dangers posed by the Jamaica Pass, and if he saw the need to patrol toward it, why then did he not see the need to defend it? The only other men that might warn of a flanking attack were five mounted officers that Nathaniel Greene paid for out of his own pocket. They were stationed at the pass itself and might have been able to sound an alarm, but they could do nothing to hinder the advance of a column of 10,000 men. A lack of manpower is also no excuse. Washington further reinforced Brooklyn on August 26, following his inspection. He was now convinced that Long Island would see the British make their "grand push," as he termed it, and he could easily have earmarked some of the reinforcements to take possession of the pass. The new units included Haslet's Delawares and Smallwood's Marylanders, some of the best men under Washington's command, who were to repay his confidence the following day. Pennsylvania riflemen under Peter Kachlein and either two or three of the independent Maryland companies are also believed to have crossed to Brooklyn on this day, along with around 100 men from John Durkee's 20th Continentals who were to form the "Rangers." Washington now had around 7,000 men on Long Island, including most of his best units.

The British plan was set quietly in motion around 2000hrs on August 26 when Clinton and the vanguard left Flatlands along the King's Road. Howe and Cornwallis followed at midnight with the bulk of the column, comprising the 1st, 2nd, 3rd and 4th Battalions of the Grenadiers, the 33rd Regiment, the First Brigade, part of the 71st Highlanders, the Guards, the 2nd, 3rd and 5th Brigades and the 49th Regiment as the rearguard. A total of 28 cannons were included in the column.

Clinton's force made slow progress, taking care to capture any civilians encountered along the way to prevent them from alerting the American forces. To keep away from the Gowanus Heights where the road swung toward them, the column cut across country at the "New Lots" and made its way to Howard's Inn at the foot of the Jamaica Pass. Here, at about 0200hrs

on August 27, the British enjoyed their first piece of good fortune. The five men paid for by Greene had posted themselves in front of the pass itself and were captured by a patrol. Clinton eagerly questioned them to see if the pass had been manned since his reconnaissance but was told that it had not. Still cautious, the British then entered Howard's Inn and woke up the owner, forcing him and his son to act as guides to the pass. Taking an old Indian pathway that skirted the pass it was found to be empty and Clinton secured it with a patrol, ready to move and occupy it fully at dawn. Two hours after taking command of the Jamaica Pass, the main column under Howe, having been able to travel more quickly in the wake of the vanguard, arrived.

Howard's Inn, where the British flanking column found suitable guides to lead them through the Jamaica Pass on the night of August 26/27. (Picture Collection, The Branch Libraries, The New York Public Library, Astor, Lenox and Tilden Foundations)

THE AMERICAN RIGHT FLANK

Two hours before Clinton's vanguard arrived at Howard's Inn, two British soldiers spotted a watermelon patch near the Red Lion Inn, where Martense Lane joined the Shore or Narrows Road, and thought it worth investigating. American pickets opened fire and a little skirmish broke out—an unusual way for the largest battle of the American War of Independence to start. The American pickets, from Hand's 1st Continentals, had been on duty for four days and were exhausted—they were replaced by Pennsylvania and New York Militia units and all was quiet for the next two or three hours until Grant sent 300 men into the pass and scattered the militia.

A warning was sent to the main American lines at Brooklyn but, incredibly, the British had penetrated the Gowanus Heights with ease. Putnam ordered Lord Stirling to take reinforcements and stop the British advance. Stirling hurried away with around 1,600 men, including the "Dandy Fifth" and the Delaware Battalion. The situation was not desperate, because there was still high ground available for the Americans to make a stand and, unknown to them, the British attack was merely a diversion. Grant would no doubt push his soldiers as far forward as he could, given this unexpected opportunity, but at the first sign of organized resistance he would halt and wait for the signal from Howe before attacking in force.

William Alexander had been turned down in his claim to be recognized as Lord Stirling, but that is nevertheless how the Americans knew him and an impressed British officer at Long Island commented that "Lord Stirling fought like a wolf." (LOC, LC-USZ62-48898)

WM SMALLWOOD

Colonel William Smallwood was on Manhattan attending a court-martial when his regiment went into battle on Long Island. The "Dandy Fifth" was renowned as one of the smartest and best regiments in the whole army. (LOC, LC-USZ62-68208 5)

Samuel Parsons, the brigadier on duty, was the first to reach the crisis point. He managed to gather a small number of the scattered guard and formed a line of 20 or so men. It was enough to stop the British temporarily and more men started to arrive: Atlee with 120 men of his Pennsylvania Musketry Battalion, Huntington's Connecticut Continentals (led by Lieutenant-Colonel Joel Clark, Huntington being ill) and Kachlein's Pennsylvania riflemen. Alarm guns were fired and the troops on Brooklyn awoke to the realization that the battle had started.

Grant's column was moving once more and approaching a bridge over an area of marshy ground. On Stirling's arrival he quickly sized up the situation and ordered Atlee to take his men forward to hold the British while he formed the Maryland and Delaware units on a ridge of land to make a more determined resistance. Atlee later reported:

I received orders from Lord Stirling to advance with my battalion and oppose the enemy's passing a morass or swamp at the foot of a fine rising ground, upon which they were first discovered, and therefore give time to our brigade to form upon the heights. This order I immediately obeyed, notwithstanding we must be exposed without any kind of cover to the great fire of the enemy's musketry and field pieces, charged with round and grapeshot, and finely situated upon the eminence above mentioned, having entire command of the ground I was ordered to occupy.

Atlee's untried men did well, standing up to fire from the British and returning it before calmly withdrawing to take position in the line formed by Stirling. The right of this line was occupied by the Marylanders, commanded by Major Mordecai Gist, followed by the Delawares under Major Thomas McDonough. Atlee's small force was to the left of these. Kachlein's riflemen were then split into two units, the first taking up skirmishing positions in front of Gist and the remainder forming next to Atlee. Huntington's men formed the left of the line.

The American line was well posted and organized, but the entire force numbered only around 1,600. Grant, who had by now been reinforced by the 42nd Regiment and two companies of Loyalists, had around 7,000. Nevertheless, holding to the plan of merely mounting a diversion, he formed his men into lines as if to assault—and then did very little. Light infantry pushed forward to near the bridge and exchanged fire with Kachlein's riflemen. The right of the British line was extended and threatened to overlap Stirling's force. Quickly the American commander ordered Atlee's and Huntington's men to move farther left. Under command of Parsons they contested ownership of what is now Battle Hill with the 23rd, 44th and elements of the 17th British regiments. The redcoats reached the hill first and checked the advance of Atlee's men with a volley, but Atlee encouraged his men to regroup and drove the British from the hill. A second British assault was repulsed and, with the Americans scrabbling among the British dead to find more cartridges, an ammunition wagon arrived just in time. A third British attack, with the support of the 42nd Regiment, was threatened but did not materialize.

Surprisingly, this little engagement at Battle Hill, in a section of the battlefield that was intended to see only a diversionary demonstration, gave the British their heaviest casualties of the day. Parsons reported of the action:

I was ordered ... to cover the left flank of our main body. This we executed though our number did at no time exceed 300 men and we were attacked three several times [actually twice] by two regiments ... and repulsed them in every attack with considerable loss. The number of dead we had collected together and the heap the enemy had made we supposed amounted to about 60. We had 12 or 14 wounded prisoners who we caused to be dressed and their wounds put in the best state our situation would admit.

Colonel John Haslet's Delawares were an imposing sight in their smart uniforms, adding a much needed dash of professionalism to Washington's army and also standing up extremely well to the rigors of battle. Their commanding officer was killed at Princeton. (Domenick D'Andrea)

The Americans had lost two or three dead officers, including Lieutenant-Colonel Caleb Parry, a personal friend of Atlee's, and a small but undetermined number of men.

The situation now developed into a stand-off. A two-gun battery under Captain Benajah Carpenter had arrived to support Stirling's line and Grant contented himself with an artillery duel that he pursued with a little too much enthusiasm—he ran through his entire day's supply of ammunition and had to send for more. Stirling's men bore the fire calmly, although it must have been terrifying, and the engagement took on far more relevance than a mere diversionary attack might have been expected to. Not only were the opposing lines drawn up "in true English taste" as one of the Marylanders would later comment, making this the first pitched battle of the war, it also provided evidence of the quality of men the Americans could put in the field.

The British tended to range between amused condescension and outright disdain for the American fighting man at this time. Grant himself had made a speech in the House of Commons stating that he could march the length of the colonies with just 5,000 men. Yet here were inexperienced Americans standing firm in the face of a fierce and sustained barrage. The Maryland soldier went on in his account of the battle:

The British then advanced within about 200 yards of us, and began a heavy fire from their cannon and mortars, for both the balls and shells flew very

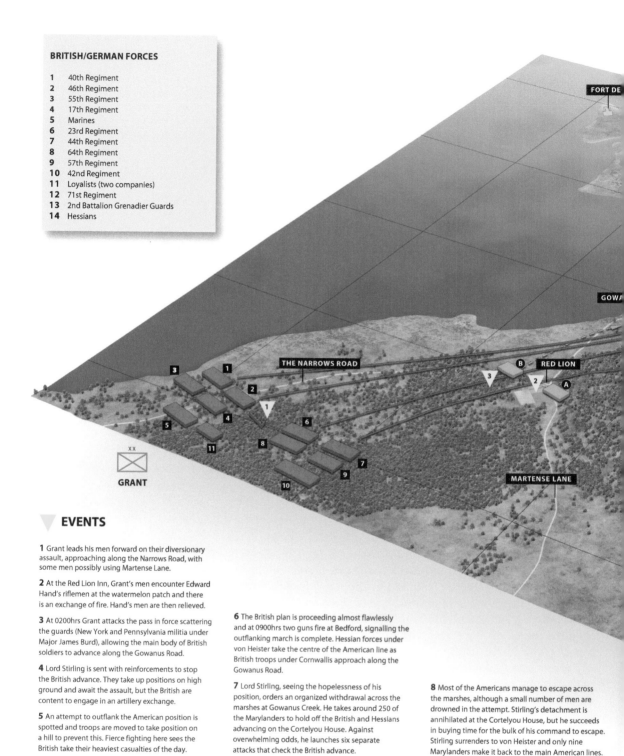

BRITISH/GERMAN FORCES

1   40th Regiment
2   46th Regiment
3   55th Regiment
4   17th Regiment
5   Marines
6   23rd Regiment
7   44th Regiment
8   64th Regiment
9   57th Regiment
10 42nd Regiment
11 Loyalists (two companies)
12 71st Regiment
13 2nd Battalion Grenadier Guards
14 Hessians

FORT DE

GOWA

THE NARROWS ROAD

RED LION

MARTENSE LANE

GRANT

▼ EVENTS

1 Grant leads his men forward on their diversionary assault, approaching along the Narrows Road, with some men possibly using Martense Lane.

2 At the Red Lion Inn, Grant's men encounter Edward Hand's riflemen at the watermelon patch and there is an exchange of fire. Hand's men are then relieved.

3 At 0200hrs Grant attacks the pass in force scattering the guards (New York and Pennsylvania militia under Major James Burd), allowing the main body of British soldiers to advance along the Gowanus Road.

4 Lord Stirling is sent with reinforcements to stop the British advance. They take up positions on high ground and await the assault, but the British are content to engage in an artillery exchange.

5 An attempt to outflank the American position is spotted and troops are moved to take position on a hill to prevent this. Fierce fighting here sees the British take their heaviest casualties of the day.

6 The British plan is proceeding almost flawlessly and at 0900hrs two guns fire at Bedford, signalling the outflanking march is complete. Hessian forces under von Heister take the centre of the American line as British troops under Cornwallis approach along the Gowanus Road.

7 Lord Stirling, seeing the hopelessness of his position, orders an organized withdrawal across the marshes at Gowanus Creek. He takes around 250 of the Marylanders to hold off the British and Hessians advancing on the Cortelyou House. Against overwhelming odds, he launches six separate attacks that check the British advance.

8 Most of the Americans manage to escape across the marshes, although a small number of men are drowned in the attempt. Stirling's detachment is annihilated at the Cortelyou House, but he succeeds in buying time for the bulk of his command to escape. Stirling surrenders to von Heister and only nine Marylanders make it back to the main American lines.

BATTLE OF LONG ISLAND, AUGUST 27, 1776: THE AMERICAN RIGHT FLANK

In the early hours of August 27, Major-General James Grant launched a diversionary attack on the American right flank. Though intended merely to distract attention from the left, where the key flanking march was taking place, this sector of the battlefield saw the fiercest fighting of the whole day

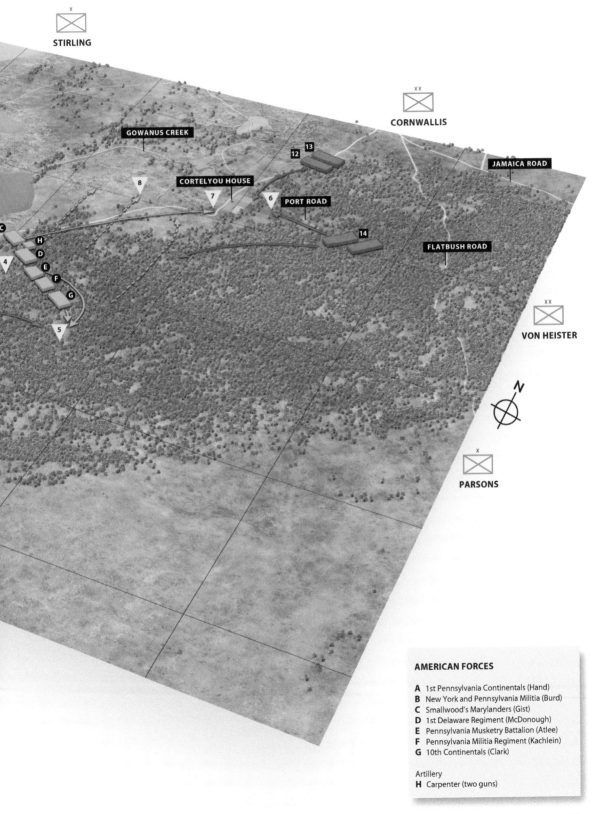

STIRLING

GOWANUS CREEK

CORNWALLIS

JAMAICA ROAD

13

12

CORTELYOU HOUSE

8

7

6 PORT ROAD

C

H

D

E

F

G

4

5

14

FLATBUSH ROAD

VON HEISTER

N

PARSONS

AMERICAN FORCES

A 1st Pennsylvania Continentals (Hand)
B New York and Pennsylvania Militia (Burd)
C Smallwood's Marylanders (Gist)
D 1st Delaware Regiment (McDonough)
E Pennsylvania Musketry Battalion (Atlee)
F Pennsylvania Militia Regiment (Kachlein)
G 10th Continentals (Clark)

Artillery
H Carpenter (two guns)

In Smallwood's absence, Major Mordecai Gist led the Marylanders at Long Island and also stepped in after Smallwood was injured at White Plains. One of his sons, States Rights (brother to Independence), fought and died as a Confederate general at the battle of Franklin in 1864. (LOC, LC-USZ62-68208 5)

fast, now and then taking off a head. Our men stood it amazingly well; not even one of them shewed a disposition to shrink. Our orders were not to fire until the enemy came within fifty yards of us, but when they perceived we stood their fire so coolly and resolutely they declined coming any nearer, altho' treble our number.

The fact that Grant had no intentions of pressing a serious attack must be borne in mind, but the courage under fire of Stirling's command, notably the Maryland and Delaware regiments, is remarkable nonetheless.

"The Delawares drew up on the side of a hill," their commander, Colonel Haslet, later wrote, "and stood upwards of four hours, with a firm, determined countenance, in close array, their colours flying, the enemy's artillery playing on them all the while, not daring to advance and attack them."

Grant's main objective, to create a diversion, had worked. Men in the Brooklyn lines and New York itself heard the lively artillery bombardment and the best reinforcements available had been drawn to the right flank. Apart from a show of movement from the Hessians in the center, nothing else seemed to be happening. Sullivan had reason to be satisfied with events when he toured the American center at Flatbush Pass. He was concerned by events on the right flank, but the calm elsewhere appears to have convinced the Americans that Grant's attack was the main thrust. Sullivan is reported to have inspected the lines at the Flatbush Pass between 0830hrs and 0900hrs. It is impossible not to wonder if it was while he was considering with some satisfaction the state of affairs along the Gowanus Heights that he heard two cannon shots from his left. He may have turned toward the village of Bedford, where the shots appeared to come from.

THE FLANKING COLUMN

At precisely 0900hrs, two cannons were fired at Bedford to signal that the flanking column had achieved its goal. A force of 10,000 was now behind the American defenses along the Gowanus Heights.

The march had not been pleasant. The threat of a sudden ambush had been a constant concern throughout the long, dark hours and the lack of sleep must have left the men exhausted by the time they reached Bedford. Captain Sir James Murray, with the 57th Regiment, commented that the march was:

As disagreeable a one as I remember to have passed in the course of my campaigning. We dragged on at the most tedious pace from sunset till 3 o'clock in the morning, halting every minute just long enough to drop asleep and to be disturbed again in order to proceed twenty yards in the same manner. The night was colder too than I remember to have felt it, so that by daybreak my stock of patience had begun to run very low.

The realization that a difficult and potentially perilous night march had been accomplished was a boost to the flagging soldiers, who now had every reason to believe that the day would be a complete success. Washington had crossed over to Brooklyn, hastening to the battle that could clearly be heard on Manhattan Island, by the time the main British column began to move again. Further reinforcements were called from New York, but it was too late for them to make any difference now. Joseph Plumb Martin was among the men

This 1852 view of Greenwood Cemetery, site of Stirling's stubborn resistance, gives a glimpse of Long Island before massive urbanization buried the bulk of the battlefield. (LOC, LC-DIG-pga-03108)

ferried over and the sights and sounds of his first battle were sobering. "We soon landed at Brooklyn upon the Island, marched up the ascent from the ferry to the plain," he wrote. "We now began to meet the wounded men, another sight I was unacquainted with, some with broken arms, some with broken legs, and some with broken heads. The sight of these a little daunted me, and made me think of home, but the sight and thought vanished together."

Samuel Miles' detachment had not detected the British march until it was too late, despite his orders to patrol out to the Jamaica Pass and despite the fact that he later insisted he had warned others of the danger posed by the undefended route behind the American defenses. By the time his men arrived the British rearguard was already passing through and he had no chance of halting the advance. With one battalion he began firing upon the baggage train, ordering his second battalion to return to warn Sullivan. The resistance had to be brief in the face of overwhelming British strength and Miles soon gave the order for his men to find their way back to the main lines at Brooklyn as best they could. Around half of the men, Miles included, were captured.

British forces were now moving into Sullivan's rear, with further elements approaching the lines at Brooklyn and still more moving in toward Stirling's position on the American right. At Flatbush Pass the Hessians began their assault. A winding path led up to the American position and thick woods reduced the value of the rifles of the waiting American marksmen, unable as they were to find targets at long range. The American position melted away as the threat from the rear materialized and by the time the Hessian forces reached the defensive works the Americans were in full retreat. Around 2,000

BATTLE OF LONG ISLAND, AUGUST 27, 1776: THE AMERICAN CENTER AND LEFT FLANK

The American defensive line along the Gowanus Heights was fatally undermined by the failure to defend the Jamaica Pass. British forces aimed to outflank the Americans by marching under cover of darkness to get behind the defensive lines. Hessian forces in the center waited for the signal that the march had been completed before beginning their attack

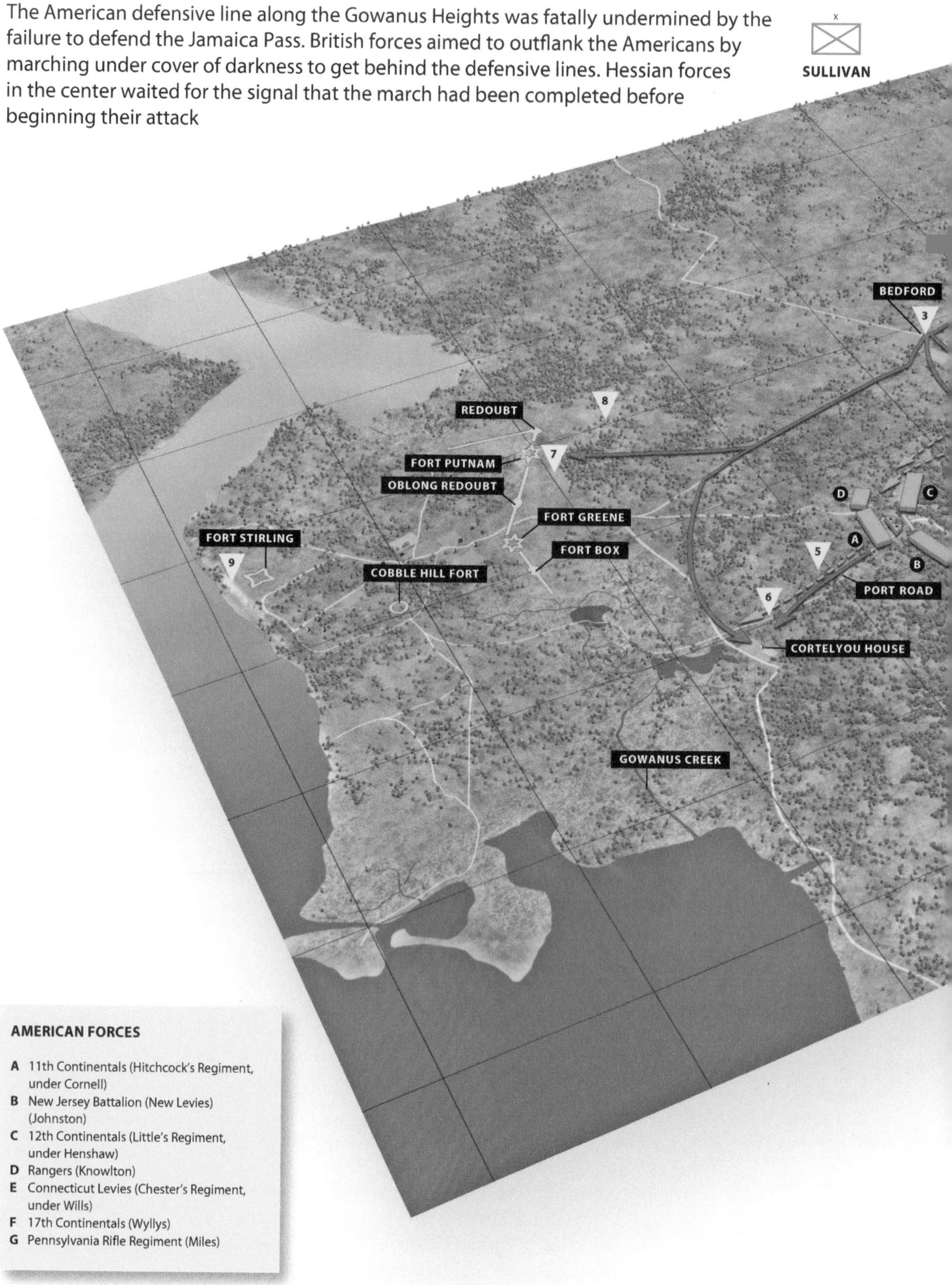

SULLIVAN

BEDFORD
3

REDOUBT
8

FORT PUTNAM
OBLONG REDOUBT
7

FORT GREENE

FORT STIRLING
9

FORT BOX
COBBLE HILL FORT

D
C
A
5
B
6
PORT ROAD

CORTELYOU HOUSE

GOWANUS CREEK

AMERICAN FORCES

A 11th Continentals (Hitchcock's Regiment, under Cornell)
B New Jersey Battalion (New Levies) (Johnston)
C 12th Continentals (Little's Regiment, under Henshaw)
D Rangers (Knowlton)
E Connecticut Levies (Chester's Regiment, under Wills)
F 17th Continentals (Wyllys)
G Pennsylvania Rifle Regiment (Miles)

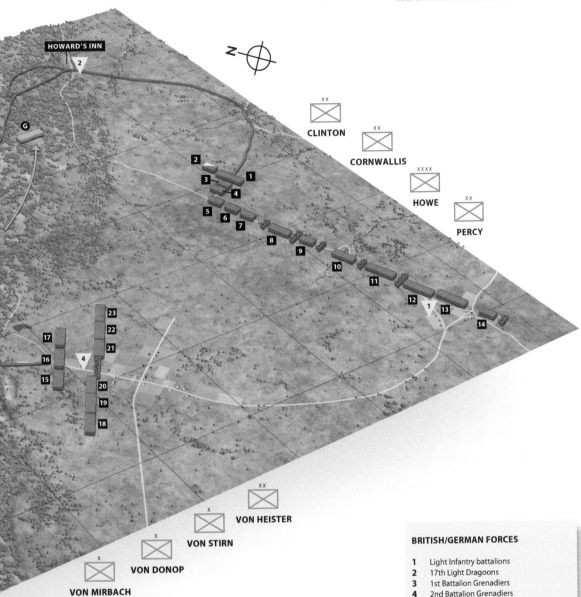

HOWARD'S INN

N

CLINTON

CORNWALLIS

HOWE

PERCY

VON HEISTER

VON STIRN

VON DONOP

VON MIRBACH

BRITISH/GERMAN FORCES

1 Light Infantry battalions
2 17th Light Dragoons
3 1st Battalion Grenadiers
4 2nd Battalion Grenadiers
5 3rd Battalion Grenadiers
6 4th Battalion Grenadiers
7 33rd Regiment
8 1st Brigade
9 71st Regiment (part of)
10 Guards
11 2nd Brigade
12 3rd Brigade
13 5th Brigade
14 49th Regiment
15 Block Grenadiers
16 3rd Battalion Grenadier von Minegrode
17 Grenadier Regiment von Lisingen
18 Fusilier Regiment von Knyphausen
19 Grenadier Regiment von Rall
20 Fusilier Regiment von Lossberg
21 Musketeer Regiment von Donop
22 Musketeer Regiment von Mirbach
23 Fusilier Regiment Erb Prinz

EVENTS

1 The British begin their flanking march, screened by the 17th Light Dragoons and spearheaded by the Light Infantry battalions.

2 Having cut across country through the New Lots, the column reaches Howard's Inn. A small party of mounted American officers is captured, removing any chance of an early warning for the Americans along the Gowanus Heights.

3 On reaching Bedford, at around 0900hrs, the British fire two shots to signal that the flanking march has been successfully completed.

4 Von Heister's Hessian Division storms the centre of the American line, which also comes under fire from elements of the flanking column, which are now operating in their rear.

5 The Americans at Flatbush Pass, numbering only around 800, retreat along the Port Road, pursued by Hessians.

6 Elements of the flanking column and of von Heister's Hessians converge on the Cortelyou House, where Lord Stirling's Marylanders stage their delaying action.

7 Parts of the British column attempt to storm the American lines at the Brooklyn Heights, but are called back by Howe.

8 Howe's starts to construct siege works on August 28.

9 Having briefly reinforced his position, Washington wisely chooses to withdraw his forces and manages to do so in good order on the night of August 29.

The heroic sacrifice of the "Dandy Fifth," led by Lord Stirling. British troops inside the Cortelyou House fire on the Americans who are holding back the advance of Cornwallis' men to give the bulk of Stirling's command time to escape across the Gowanus Creek. (Picture Collection, The Branch Libraries, The New York Public Library, Astor, Lenox and Tilden Foundations)

men were attempting to reach the safety of the lines at Brooklyn, often finding themselves caught between British and Hessian units. Many surrendered, some were bayoneted, and some chose to find a quiet spot and attempt to hide until the immediate danger had passed. Only on the right flank did organized resistance continue.

By 1100hrs Stirling was aware of the threat to his rear and Grant was pushing forward with more determination. The time had come to withdraw, even though he had received no official order to retreat. In fact, Stirling had left it too late. Cornwallis, with the 71st Regiment and the Second Grenadiers, had already taken control of the Gowanus Road, the road to Brooklyn. Hessian units were also moving along the Gowanus Heights and converging with Cornwallis—there was no clear route back to safety.

Stirling made the decision to take a contingent of the Marylanders and attempt to hold off the advancing British and Hessians while the remainder of his command retreated across the marshlands at Gowanus Creek. With around 260 men he headed straight for Cornwallis, meeting him at the Cortelyou House (also known as the 'Old Stone House'). Stirling's stand against Grant was already the single positive in what was rapidly becoming a disastrously negative morning. Now he would elevate his reputation, and that of the Marylanders with him, to almost mythic proportions with a quite staggering display of bravery. Against superior and rapidly growing numbers Stirling ordered his men to attack. This they did, repeatedly charging Cornwallis' men and holding them back long enough for the rest of his command to make their way into the marshes, where most of them struggled to safety, although several men drowned. Of the Marylanders, only nine escaped death, injury or capture. Stirling himself surrendered to the Hessian General von Heister. Washington, from a vantage point at Cobble Hill Fort, watched the actions of the Marylanders and is reputed to have cried out: "What brave fellows I must lose this day!" Unseen to Washington, the men under Parsons at Battle Hill had also been lost. Left behind when Stirling withdrew they were completely isolated and, belatedly attempting to retreat, they found their way to the marsh cut off by Cornwallis. Almost all of the men were captured. Parsons himself, however, was able to hide along with seven men in a swamp and reached the American lines at Brooklyn the following morning.

The Americans had suffered a shattering loss. They had been completely outmaneuvered by Howe and their defensive lines, intended to inflict heavy losses on the British, had failed completely. Yet the defeat could have easily been far worse. As the British flanking column dispersed to attack various targets, several units pushed close to the main defenses at Brooklyn. In Howe's own words, the Grenadiers and 33rd Regiment "pursued numbers of the rebels ... so close to their principal redoubt, and with such eagerness to attack it by storm, that it required repeated orders to prevail upon them to desist. …" Howe's reasons for insisting on halting his men have been long debated. He would state that he was unwilling to risk the losses that might stem from a frontal assault, yet in his report to Germain he went on to say: "Had they been permitted to go on, it is my opinion they would have carried the redoubt."

Had the lines at Brooklyn been breached there would have been no alternative for the Americans but to surrender entirely, giving the British complete control of Long Island and removing around 9,000 rebel soldiers, including Washington, from the Continental Army. It is possible that the entire revolutionary cause would have died right there. Clinton commented that "had the attempt [on the Brooklyn lines] been made – the completest success would most likely have been the consequence."

The extent of the British victory as it stood has also been hotly debated. Initial reports and many early histories put American losses at over 3,000, but given the numbers of men that were posted at the Gowanus Heights, and the numbers who made it safely back to the Brooklyn defenses, this number looks inflated. There was also talk of massacres and blood-letting on a huge scale, particularly by the Hessians, but, although there were incidences of soldiers being killed while attempting to surrender, there was no large-scale butchery. Most modern historians favor an assessment of around 1,000 total losses on the American side, with only 200 or so killed or wounded. Howe reported his losses as 61 killed, with 267 wounded and 31 taken prisoner.

There is also a question about the British plan, so flawless at first glance. American generals are criticized for failing to defend the Jamaica Pass, but why should Howe be forgiven for sounding his signal cannons, and thus alerting the Americans to his presence, at Bedford? If his column had simply continued marching up to the Brooklyn lines they would have been able to trap all of the forces along the Gowanus Heights. Bedford was a curious place to choose to halt, being behind only one of the American positions, at the Bedford Pass itself.

The retreat at Gowanus. Despite the treacherous terrain only a handful of men drowned on the scramble to the safety of the Brooklyn lines. (NA, 111-SC-96741)

THE CHARGE OF THE MARYLANDERS AT GOWANUS, AUGUST 27, 1776 (pp. 52–53)

The situation for the American right flank on Long Island was perilous in the extreme as British troops under Cornwallis pressed towards their rear. Realizing that an organized withdrawal along the Gowanus Road was now impossible, the order was given for the Americans to retreat across the Gowanus Creek.

To buy time for the retreating men, Major-General William Alexander (Lord Stirling) took a section of Maryland's "Dandy Fifth" to stage a delaying action. They met the advancing British at the Cortelyou House (1) on the Gowanus Road.

The number of Marylanders involved is debated. Conventional history puts it at 400, but this seems inflated given the resulting losses from the clash with the British (256 killed, wounded and captured, with nine making their way back to the American lines at Brooklyn).

What is certain is that Cornwallis had already taken possession of the Cortelyou House and had placed a 6-pdr in front of it (2) by the time Stirling arrived. The Americans would be forced to advance in the face of destructive firepower.

Stirling himself (3) and Major Mordecai Gist (4) led the Marylanders, who lined up in two ranks to advance. Multiple attacks were pressed home (legend has it that the Marylanders

marched forward six times), with the field becoming littered with the wounded of both the Americans (5) and the British troops involved, including men from Fraser's Highlanders, the 71st Regiment (6).

Along with the 1st Delaware Regiment, the Marylanders were prized as the elite of Washington's army and their quality showed as they retained their discipline despite the hopelessness of the task, facing around 2,000 British and Hessian soldiers. They were also (again, along with the Delawares) one of the few American units to be issued with bayonets, which they made good use of here.

Despite the odds, they actually twice drove the British from the Cortelyou House, though on each occasion they were quickly forced to withdraw themselves and as their losses mounted it became impossible to mount further attacks. Ordering his men to find their way back to the American lines, Stirling himself sought out a Hessian to surrender to, rather than the British.

The sacrifice of the "Maryland 400," as they are remembered, was not in vain, as they held up the British long enough for the bulk of the Americans on the right flank to escape through the marshlands to Brooklyn.

Howe's decision to call off his attack just when the Americans seemed to be within his grasp demands an explanation. Perhaps the most reasonable is that offered by Howe himself. His report to Germain continued with the statement that: "… as it was apparent the lines must have been ours at a very cheap rate by regular approaches, I would not risk the loss that might have been sustained in the assault." Not wanting to risk serious casualties is a valid reason to halt an attack, and the British column had been on the move since around 2000hrs the previous night. Ignoring the disappointment of his men, Howe set up camp within view of the American lines and started to build siege works the following day.

Historians have offered many more reasons for Howe's decision. Was he overcautious? Had he suddenly become incapable of daring moves? Did he believe the battle was already won and that there was no way for Washington to escape? Most plausible is the idea that he wanted to deliver a blow to American morale—but not too serious a blow. Had he administered a sharp lesson and then allowed the Americans to escape, mindful that reconciliation was the ultimate goal? Whatever his reasons, the battle of Long Island would be remembered as a missed opportunity, "a great might-have-been" as the historian Jeremy Black has written. John Keegan, considering the nature of 18th-century warfare, has also offered the suggestion that Howe might have simply been waiting for Washington to do the decent thing and surrender.

Washington had no such thoughts as he regrouped following the shock of August 27. He had already brought reinforcements over in the morning (three regiments of Connecticut levies from Wadsworth's Brigade, the 19th Continentals of Alexander McDougall's Brigade and the 2nd New York County Battalion along with a regiment of New York Militia from Scott's Brigade, Scott himself also moving to Brooklyn at this time). Washington called further reinforcements over on August 28 and prepared to make a stand. The 3rd and 5th Pennsylvania Battalions of Mifflin's Brigade came over from Harlem Heights, together with the 14th Continentals, the "Marblehead Regiment" of Massachusetts. This reinforcement was a potentially huge mistake. The defenses at Brooklyn had no easy line of retreat and bringing reinforcements over was once more simply increasing the scale of the inevitable defeat that would follow. Henry P. Johnston, in his exhaustive account of the battle, commented of Washington that "He had on that side [Brooklyn] the largest and best part of his army." The forces at Brooklyn numbered around 9,500 and the British would never have a better chance of destroying the Main Army.

The situation could hardly have been grimmer. Heavy rains lashed the rebels for the two days following the battle. "You may judge of our situation," wrote John Morin Scott of the situation in the lines, "subject to almost incessant rains, without baggage or tents, and almost without victuals or drink, and in some parts of the lines the men were standing up to their middles in water." The weather had one benefit—unfavorable winds prevented British ships from entering the East River and cutting Long Island off from Manhattan.

Amazingly, Washington and his army would escape. On the morning of August 29 the British were found to be a mere 600 yards from the American lines—another 24 hours of approaching zigzag trenches would put the American lines within range of musket fire. Washington saw that his position could not be held and he made the decision to attempt an evacuation, but in the face of an enemy that outnumbered him two to one and was, presumably,

Having divided his army, Washington worked a minor miracle to reunite it on Manhattan, pulling off a daring evacuation of Long Island on the night of August 29. (LOC, LC-USZ62-96920)

watching him very closely, this might have seemed an impossible task. It would also have to be carried off in a single night if a portion of the garrison of Brooklyn was not to be irretrievably left behind. Manhattan was scoured for boats and the pressure was intense. The order that was sent to Assistant Quartermaster Hugh Hughes, on Manhattan, did not leave room for any doubt. Hughes was to "impress every kind of water craft from Hell Gate on the Sound to Spuyten Duyvil Creek that could be kept afloat and that had either sails or oars, and have them all in the east harbor of the city by dark."

Washington's decision to evacuate on the 29th, having steadily reinforced his position at Brooklyn through the 27th and 28th, has proved a contentious topic, with some claiming it highlighted his inexperience and indecision at this crisis point. Washington certainly was inexperienced, but his actions here are wholly consistent with his stated aims. He hoped to force the British to make a frontal assault on prepared positions, giving him the chance to inflict serious losses that Howe would find impossible to replace. Documents from a meeting Washington undertook with his officers on August 29 show them to be all too aware of the weakness of their position, referring as it does to the danger of being cut off by enemy shipping and the weakness of the entrenchments between the forts and redoubts. Even the danger of keeping the army divided was mentioned, but all of these elements existed before the battle had started and yet Washington had continued to reinforce. The only element that had changed by the morning of August 29 was the fact that the British siege works were clearly visible. The British were not going to mount the frontal assault Washington had hoped for and would inevitably take his position in due course. Evacuation was the only possible response and it would have to take place within 24 hours or the British would be within range of his lines.

The organization of the American evacuation of Long Island was remarkable given the conditions. Mifflin was to command a 1,000-man rearguard and the regiments began to file down the Ferry Road at 2000hrs on August 29. Campfires were left burning and the entrenchments were

Perhaps most remarkable about the retreat from Long Island was the fact that the Americans were able to bring their artillery safely off as well, testament both to their resourcefulness and the complacency of the British. (LOC, LC-USZ62-3919)

manned until the last possible moment in an attempt to fool the British, but although discipline remained good the entire undertaking could have come apart on at least three occasions.

An order from Washington, carried by Alexander Scammell and informing all regiments in the lines to withdraw to the crossing point, caused confusion when it was incorrectly delivered to Mifflin. Confused, Mifflin withdrew his men, only to be confronted by an appalled Washington, who feared that the removal of the rearguard might spell disaster. In a display of discipline and no little courage, Mifflin marched his men back to their place in the trenches.

The British also came close to discovering the evacuation when a patrol led by Captain John Montresor discovered the Brooklyn lines in front of them were empty, but no action was taken. Finally, a black slave was sent to warn the British, but he first encountered Hessians, who did not understand what he was saying.

As dawn broke, only a few regiments remained in the lines and a thick fog descended as if to shield them from view. Mifflin's rearguard finally got a genuine order to withdraw and what is sometimes referred to as the "American Dunkirk" had been completed. Whether or not Howe had been negligent, complacent or had even allowed Washington's army to escape are interesting points to debate, but the fact is the Americans would fight another day.

THE CLEARING OF NEW YORK

History looks back on the evacuation of Long Island as an impressive achievement and modern perceptions are inevitably colored by the knowledge that the colonies would eventually prevail in their struggle for independence. At the time, however, it was a cause of great despondency for the Americans. Washington's army was badly demoralized and there was a feeling that they had been let down by their leaders.

"Upon the whole," wrote Daniel Brodhead, part of Miles' Regiment that had been patrolling out toward the Jamaica Pass, "less generalship never was shown in any army since the art of war was understood." He conceded that the evacuation of Long Island had been "well conducted," but he was obviously feeling the sting of blame attached to his unit for the failure to prevent or detect the British flanking move at the Jamaica Pass. "I understand that Gen. Sullivan has taken the liberty to charge our brave and good Col. Miles, with the ill success of the day," he continued, "but give me leave to say, that if Gen' Sullivan & the rest of the Gen'ls on Long Island, had been as vigilant & prudent as him, we might, & in all probability would have cut off Clinton's brigade."

Washington was aware of the dampened spirits among his men and the General Orders of August 31 were at pains to reassure them that "... the retreat from Long-Island was made by the unanimous advice of all the general officers, not from any doubts of the spirit of the troops. ..."

This view of New York City, an engraving of a drawing made by Captain Thomas Howdell of the Royal Artillery in 1768, is taken from the modern-day intersection of Henry and Montgomery streets on Manhattan, looking southwest. Across the East River, to the extreme left of the image, is Long Island. (LOC, LC-USZ62-19363)

Washington was telling a different tale to Congress. On September 2 he wrote: "Till of late I had no doubt in my own mind of defending this place, nor should I have yet, if the men would do their duty, but this I despair of. It is painful, and extremely grating to me, to give such unfavorable accounts; but it would be criminal to conceal the truth at so critical a juncture."

Washington's comments were probably aimed squarely at the thousands of militia who were streaming away from the army at this point. Believing that a standing army was the only solution to the problem of fluctuating numbers he often took pains to criticize the militia. The actual performance of his men on Long Island had been commendable—forced to retreat only because of a disastrous outflanking that was the fault of their commanding officers, they had performed well, even heroically, in the only section of the battlefield where they had been given the chance to confront the enemy under normal circumstances. Furthermore, they had evacuated Long Island with great discipline given the tension and fear of discovery by the British.

The loss of Long Island and, particularly, the Brooklyn Heights put the city of New York under threat. However, although some inhabitants wrote of their daily fear of the British bombarding the town, this was never going to happen. More likely was another attempt to outflank the Main Army by landing troops on Manhattan or even beyond Kingsbridge, in Westchester County. The loss of Brooklyn removed one of the keys to the American plan to deny access to the East River to British shipping—the guns of Fort Stirling.

"News from America, or the Patriots in the Dumps." A triumphant Lord North reads of the success of British forces in America while "America" slumps at his feet in misery. (LOC, LC-USZ61-80)

Washington set to work preparing to defend Manhattan, but his planning revealed that he had still not fully appreciated the dangers of dividing his army. Brigades were reorganized to take into account the losses on Long Island and three divisions were formed, under Putnam, Spencer and Heath. Putnam's five brigades (those of Parsons, Scoot, Glover, Fellows and Silliman) guarded the city and the East River. Spencer's division comprised McDougall's, Wadsworth's, Douglas' and Chester's brigades, as well as a newly organized brigade under Colonel Paul Dudley Sargent. With Greene's ill health continuing, his two brigades (Nixon's and Heard's) also fell under Spencer's command. This division connected with Putnam's to extend the line to Horn's Hook and Harlem. Heath's Division, consisting of just two brigades (Mifflin's and George Clinton's), was posted at Kingsbridge and on the Westchester shore. The need to protect the entire East River shoreline meant that Washington's shaken army was stretched over more than 14 miles. Defenses on the Hudson River were still composed of batteries at Paulus Hook and forts Washington and Lee, with the sunken hulks across the river between them.

Even while this new defensive alignment was being put in place, debate was raging over whether New York could or *should* be defended. The same problems that faced the garrison of Long Island now applied to that on Manhattan—a bold British move to land troops in Westchester would trap the entire Main Army on Manhattan. Nathaniel Greene was particularly vociferous in his opposition to holding the city: "The City and Island of New York are no objects to us," he wrote to Washington on September 5. "… Two-thirds of the property of the City of New York and the suburbs belong to the tories. We have no very great reason to run any considerable risk for its defense … I would give it as my opinion that a general and speedy retreat is absolutely necessary, and that the honor and interest of America require it. I would burn the city."

Congress was set against any destruction of the city, believing it could quickly be retaken even if it fell into British hands (a misconception that would be borne out by the fact that British troops did not eventually quit New York until 1783) and Washington resolved to stay put.

The Main Army's commander-in-chief would probably have been a little surprised to find that the mood of the British was scarcely more buoyant than his own. There was resentment among both officers and men that the victory at Long Island had not been decisive. Admiral Howe chose this point to make another attempt to find a peaceful resolution to the war. Inviting Benjamin Franklin, John Adams and Edward Rutledge to join him for a conference on September 11, he expressed his sadness at the state of affairs and professed his great affection for the American people. Franklin, regardless of the gravity of the situation and the genuine sentiments being expressed by Lord Howe, gave one of his glib replies that apparently saddened the admiral and the conference came to nothing.

Not everyone in the British contingent saw the current situation as a cause for grave concern, of course. Lord Percy, who had previously commented that the British Army was "… so small that we cannot even afford a victory," now wrote of the Americans that, "Everything seems to be over with them, and I flatter myself now that this campaign will put a total end to the war."

KIP'S BAY

Moving troops to Manhattan was the next task for William Howe, and this time he would be making an opposed landing, in contrast to the straightforward transfer from Staten Island to Long Island. The nature of sea transport must also be considered. Many write freely of the British mastery

This portrayal of the British landing on Manhattan bears no resemblance to the event at Kip's Bay, although it does appear to be unopposed, as the actual landing turned out to be. (LOC, LC-USZ62-45372)

"Mrs Murray's Strategy." This painting, by E. Percy Moran, brings the legend to life. Howe did spend time with his officers at the house of Mrs Robert Murray, but she was renowned for her hospitality and it is highly unlikely she had ulterior motives. (LOC, LC-USZC4-6507)

of the seas as if this gave them the ability to land wherever and whenever they chose. It did give them a great advantage over a land-based force, but it was also subject to tides and weather conditions and was a time-consuming logistical operation even when all went smoothly. Preparations for the landing on Manhattan were therefore not completed until September 15. Dismissing the idea of a move into the back portion of Manhattan, or into Westchester County, Howe proposed to land at Kip's Bay, a point to the rear of the bulk of Washington's forces. Three warships would make a diversionary expedition up the North River as part of this operation.

Henry Clinton, free as ever with his criticism, did not approve of the plan. Having suggested one of his customary moves to get behind the enemy (by landing at Morrisania and moving to occupy the heights of Fordham, thus preventing an evacuation of Manhattan via Kingsbridge) he was scornful of Howe's plan. "In short," he wrote prior to the landing, "I like it not. No diversion, no demonstration but what a child would see through, little prospect of victory without buying it dear, some apprehension of receiving— what we might have given—a defeat in detail."

The delay in moving on Manhattan had also given Washington time to have a change of heart. On September 7 he had decided to leave a garrison of 5,000 men in the city and remove the bulk of his army to the Harlem Heights. By the time Howe was ready to move, therefore, the majority of Washington's army was already beyond the reach of the planned landing at Kip's Bay. Furthermore, on September 12, a council of war came to the conclusion that holding New York could serve no purpose and the remaining garrison was ordered to evacuate as well. This started immediately and was ongoing as the British made their move. Landing craft had been assembled over the preceding days, accompanied by five warships, the *Rose*, *Roebuck*, *Phoenix*, *Orpheus* and *Carysfort*. On September 15 they prepared to make the landing at Kip's Bay.

There is some confusion over what happened next. Henry Clinton, leading the assault despite his misgivings, believed that a delay in setting the landing craft on their way fooled the American defenders into thinking that a different landing area had been chosen, forcing them to move from their defenses. Douglas, commanding the Americans at Kip's Bay, stated that the five British warships took up a position to his left ("within a musket shot") requiring him to relocate his defenders. The line they took up was very lightly fortified, being little more than a shallow ditch with the earth thrown up before it. Into this ditch moved Douglas' men, including Joseph Plumb Martin. As the British landing craft were filled, Martin apparently grew bored and started to explore his surroundings, sitting down in a nearby barn and reading some papers that were scattered there.

A Hessian lieutenant, part of the landing force, commented on events that followed: "Last Sunday," he wrote, "we landed under the thundering rattle of five men-of-war." The combined firepower of all five British warships was unleashed to cover the advance of around 4,000 men in 84 landing craft. Martin believed that his "head might go with the sound." Douglas' militia had no option but to crouch in their ditch and wait for the bombardment to finish, but the flimsy nature of the works and the ferocity of the bombardment ("as heavy a cannonade perhaps as ever was from no more ships," in Douglas' words) began to collapse the entrenchment and the militia were forced to withdraw.

Light infantry, Hessian Jägers and Donop's Grenadiers comprised the landing force, under Clinton and Cornwallis, and they now had an opportunity to advance quickly across Manhattan to bottle up the remaining 3,500 or so Americans still in the process of evacuating the city of New York. Panic had gripped the rebel militia and they could not be rallied so there was effectively no opposition to the sizable British force that had just landed on Manhattan.

Washington, riding to the sound of the guns from his position at Harlem Heights, attempted to rally the fugitives, but the panic spread and infected regiments sent up as reinforcements. It was not only militiamen who fled, but experienced regiments, including Prescott's 7th Colonial Infantry who had stood at Bunker Hill. Legend has it that Washington, shocked by the rout of his men, sat dejected on his horse and narrowly escaped capture by advancing Hessians. Whether or not this is true, the commander-in-chief was understandably dismayed at his inability to rally his troops and make an organized withdrawal.

The situation for the remaining men in New York was now dire. Israel Putnam set off for the city to inform them of the danger. Putnam's aide, Major Aaron Burr, revealed that he knew the area well and believed he could lead the men to safety, which he did on a grueling 12-mile march on what was an extremely hot day. Burr's efforts might have been in vain, however, had the British moved quickly after securing their beachhead, but Clinton was under orders to secure the area and await reinforcements before advancing. It took several hours before these reinforcements arrived, much to Clinton's disgust. Howe and several fellow officers were then apparently detained at the house of Mrs Robert Murray, who offered wine and cakes and was such an entertaining hostess that the commander-in-chief stayed at her house for two hours. The legend grew that Mrs Murray acted deliberately to stall the British advance—once more it is impossible to know how much of "Mrs Murray's strategy" is fact and how much romance, but it is undeniable that Howe let a large body of Americans slip though his fingers once more.

The negative aspects of this narrow escape seem to have made more impression on the Americans than the positive. The army was becoming divided, with the New Englanders now subject to scorn from those representing other states. Washington himself referred to the troops (from Connecticut and Massachusetts) who ran from the British as "disgraceful and dastardly." The men under bombardment from the British fleet could not, however, have been expected to remain in their positions and, once started, a disorganized retreat can quickly turn into a panic. The Americans were lacking experience (in Piers Mackesy's words they were "raw men, whose military spirit, far from being broken, had not yet been created"), but so far the British had not punished them as severely as they might. In fact, the weather was causing more misery among the American ranks than the British. Having suffered through an unusually hot day, the exhausted men of Putnam's column collapsed to sleep under a heavy downpour and a sudden, chilling drop in temperature.

The revolution was going badly when British troops entered the city of New York on September 16. There was no doubt relief among the remaining inhabitants (around a third of the population having left town until the situation settled) that the feared bombardment by the British had never materialized, but there was also a sizable contingent of Loyalists who were genuinely pleased to see the return of Royal authority. Among these was the Reverend Shewkirk, who offered an interesting insight into the recent events when viewed from a different perspective by exclaiming that "The king's flag was put up again in the fort, and the rebels' taken down. And thus, the city was delivered from those usurpers who had oppressed it so long."

THE BATTLE OF HARLEM HEIGHTS

If the Americans needed a boost to their flagging morale, they were to get one on the very day that British troops entered New York. From strong lines on the Harlem Heights, Washington dispatched Knowlton's Rangers to scout out the British position. The Rangers had originally been a group of around 100 men from Durkee's 20th Continentals that accompanied Thomas Knowlton to Long Island. The unit now consisted of volunteers from

Men of the Black Watch fall back in the face of the American advance at Harlem Heights. This small-scale skirmish gave the Americans a much-needed boost to their self-esteem. (LOC, LC-USZ62-48362)

Connecticut, Massachusetts and Rhode Island and numbered around 120. Its captains included Nathan Hale, who was to earn fame after being executed following his capture on a spying mission.

The Rangers struck off for the Bloomingdale Heights and headed towards the British positions. The units they encountered on the Bloomingdale Road were the British Light Infantry and the 42nd Highlanders. The 2nd and 3rd Battalions of the Light Infantry, together with the Black Watch, quickly responded by moving out to confront the American scouts. Some accounts now state that Knowlton immediately drew his force back behind a stone wall, others that a "few rounds" were fired before retiring to the wall, but the accounts are consistent on what happened next. Eight or nine shots per man were delivered into the advancing British before Knowlton, seeing that he was about to be outflanked, ordered a withdrawal. The Rangers left about 10 dead and wounded at the stone wall.

Washington had written to Congress that morning, reporting that, "We are now encamped with the main body of the army on the Heights of Harlem, where I should hope the enemy would meet with a defeat in case of an attack, if the generality of our troops would behave with tolerable bravery. But experience, to my extreme affliction, has convinced me that this is rather to be wished for than expected." Washington was also no doubt ruing the large quantity of supplies and "most of our heavy cannon" that had been left in New York.

The letter was sent before Washington was informed that enemy soldiers were advancing on the American positions. The Rangers were continuing to retire in good order and soon reached the American lines on the Harlem Heights. The British Light Infantry could now be seen on the Bloomingdale Heights, while in between the two elevated positions was the "Hollow Way," which extended into the Plains of Harlem. To the embarrassment of the

Americans, someone in the British force now sounded a hunting horn, as if pursuing nothing more dangerous than a fox. Washington, though, judged that the British must now be some way from their main body. He therefore ordered the Rangers, together with three of the newly arrived Virginia companies, under Major Leitch, to attempt to get around the British flank and take up a position in their rear. A diversionary force of 150 volunteers, led by Lieutenant-Colonel Archibald Crary, advanced boldly down into the Hollow Way to occupy the attention of the British. The redcoats, unable to resist such a small group, advanced quickly down the slope into the Hollow Way. The two lines exchanged long-range fire while the flanking force moved unsuspected toward the British rear. Unfortunately for the Americans, the flanking march was not completed when the Rangers and Virginians broke cover and their attack was therefore in the flank of the British rather than the rear. Still, it forced a hasty retreat and the Americans pressed their advantage, chasing the British back up the slope onto the Bloomingdale Heights.

At this point Leitch and Knowlton, leading the flanking party, were shot in quick succession and both fell mortally wounded. The junior officers pressed on the advance and Washington reinforced them—nine Maryland companies seem to have pushed forward—and the Americans now numbered

Although arsonists were blamed at the time for the New York fire, it could easily have started by accident. Had the wind changed direction the entire town might have been destroyed. (LOC, LC-USZ62-45333)

between 1,500 and 1,800. A charge dislodged the now-outnumbered British from their position and pushed them farther back until they were themselves reinforced by artillery and Hessian forces, including the Jägers.

A brief stalemate ensued as the sides exchanged fire, but the British units ran short of ammunition and were compelled to retreat once more. Having pushed their enemy close to the main British encampment, and with the danger of the tables being turned once more as reinforcements began to appear, Washington recalled his men, who gave a hearty cheer before marching back to their lines.

What was actually little more than a prolonged skirmish had an effect on the Americans out of all proportion to its size (Howe claimed to have lost 14 dead and around 70 wounded, while American losses included around 25 dead and 50 wounded). Washington's men had faced British soldiers and forced them to retreat several times. If there had been any aura of invincibility about the British and Hessian soldiers, the battle of Harlem Heights went some way to dispelling it. Washington possibly regretted the harsh words of the letter he had dispatched just before joining the action and the Americans finally had something more than brave defeats and miraculous retreats to consider. This, however small, was a victory, one that "... inspirited our troops prodigiously," as Washington wrote to General Schuyler. The action was also significant in that it involved men from Connecticut, Maryland, Virginia and Rhode Island, putting an end, for now at least, to the dangerous factionalism that had been prevalent.

Nathan Hale was on a spying mission for Washington when he was captured in the aftermath of the New York fire. He is reputed to have stated at his execution that "my only regret is that I have but one life to give for my country." (LOC, LC-USZ62-3754)

Howe now settled into one of the curious reposes that punctuated his 1776 campaign. A letter to Germain on September 25 revealed that he did not think much more was possible. Washington was well posted at the Harlem Heights and the position was too strong to attack. The only activity since the battle of Harlem Heights had been the disastrous fire that broke out in New York on September 21. Believed by most to have been started deliberately (Howe reported that several arsonists had been caught in the act), the fire destroyed a quarter of the city. "It spread so quickly," wrote the Reverend Shewkirk, "that all what was done was but of little effect; if one was in one street and looked about, it broke out already again in another street above; and thus it raged all the night, and till about noon." Tracking down those responsible (if indeed it had been arson) does not seem to have been possible, despite Howe's comments—Shewkirk writing in his diary that about 200 men were arrested on suspicion of involvement, but "... on examination, the most men were as fast discharged."

WHITE PLAINS

Howe's concerns about the American defenses at the Harlem Heights were not without foundation. In fact, Washington might have been making his defenses too formidable. If he simply hoped to stage more Bunker Hills until the British ran out of men, Howe was not about to oblige.

The Americans had constructed three lines on the heights, the central line being the strongest, including as it did four redoubts. Fort Washington also featured prominently in the works—it was believed to be impregnable. Howe built his own defensive lines in front of New York, but whether this was to signal the end of offensive operations or to make the city more defensible by a smaller force, allowing him to strike at Washington again, remained to be seen. Howe had, in fact, decided to maneuver Washington out of his strong position. He would threaten to sever Washington's communications with Connecticut and would face him in battle "if possible." This is a telling remark—it showed that the notion of destroying Washington's army was now of secondary importance to simply driving him out of New York.

Howe was finally to reach beyond the American position and genuinely threaten their rear, but the chosen landing place, Throg's Neck, was an unexpected one. It did not seem to be an advantageous place to land troops, being easily defended. The Americans guarded a causeway and the fords through which an army could reach the mainland and William Duer, at the New York Provincial Congress, commented that "Had they [the British] pushed their imaginations to discover the worst place, they could not have succeeded better than they have done."

The passage through the potentially hazardous Hell Gate had cost Admiral Howe just one ship (with the loss of three men and three 6-pdr field guns), despite the notoriously difficult waters and the fact that a fog had descended over the British vessels. Troops duly landed at Throg's Neck on October 12, but an attempt to move out quickly from the landing point and secure the bridge to the mainland (Throg's Neck actually became an island at high tide) was foiled by the Americans, who had already removed the planks on the bridge. A guard of 25 riflemen was in place and peppered the British column at the bridge, while a further British party was halted at a ford by another small guarding force. Washington ordered reinforcements to the guards around Throg's Neck and there followed a five-day delay while supplies were landed.

The Americans had already delayed moving their main force perhaps longer than was wise, but Washington finally decided to leave Manhattan Island on October 16. The council of war that had agreed a move was necessary had also made the decision to leave a garrison at Fort Washington. Exactly why is uncertain—the hope of preventing British ships from moving up the Hudson by combining the firepower of forts Washington and Lee had already been proven vain on numerous occasions. (As recently as October 9 it had been demonstrated once more, when two British frigates moved without difficulty up the Hudson.) The 2,800 men left at the fort (around 1,200 originally but quickly reinforced) were isolated and unsuited to the task at hand. If they were to hold the outlying fortifications they were too few. If they were to hold just the fort itself, they were too many. The belief that the fort was impregnable obviously played a part in the decision, and the confidence of Nathaniel Greene that it could be held or, at the worst, evacuated whenever necessary, swayed Washington. It would prove to be a huge mistake.

The perils of Hell Gate—with fierce, swirling currents and outcrops of jagged rock. The British ships that navigated it on October 12 had to do so under the extra handicap of a thick fog. (LOC, LC-USZ62-132532)

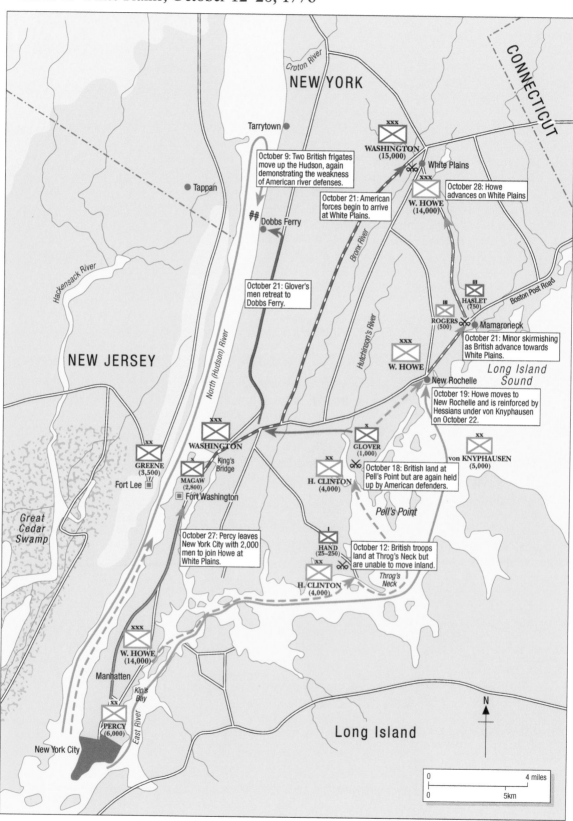

CONNECTICUT

NEW YORK

Croton River

Tarrytown

WASHINGTON
(15,000)
White Plains

October 9: Two British frigates move up the Hudson, again demonstrating the weakness of American river defenses.

October 21: American forces begin to arrive at White Plains.

Tappan

October 28: Howe advances on White Plains

W. HOWE
(14,000)

Dobbs Ferry

Bronx River

October 21: Glover's men retreat to Dobbs Ferry.

Hackensack River

HASLET
(750)

Boston Post Road

ROGERS
(500)   Mamaroneck

October 21: Minor skirmishing as British advance towards White Plains.

NEW JERSEY

North (Hudson) River

Hutchinson's River

W. HOWE

Long Island Sound

New Rochelle

October 19: Howe moves to New Rochelle and is reinforced by Hessians under von Knyphausen on October 22.

GREENE
(3,500)

WASHINGTON

King's Bridge

GLOVER
(1,000)

von KNYPHAUSEN
(5,000)

Fort Lee

MAGAW
(2,800)
Fort Washington

H. CLINTON
(4,000)

October 18: British land at Pell's Point but are again held up by American defenders.

Pell's Point

Great Cedar Swamp

October 27: Percy leaves New York City with 2,000 men to join Howe at White Plains.

HAND
(25–250)

October 12: British troops land at Throg's Neck but are unable to move inland.

Throg's Neck

H. CLINTON
(4,000)

W. HOWE
(14,000)

Manhattan

Kip's Bay

PERCY
(6,000)

East River

N

New York City

Long Island

| 0 | | 4 miles |
| 0 | | 5km |

White Plains, October 28–November 10, 1776

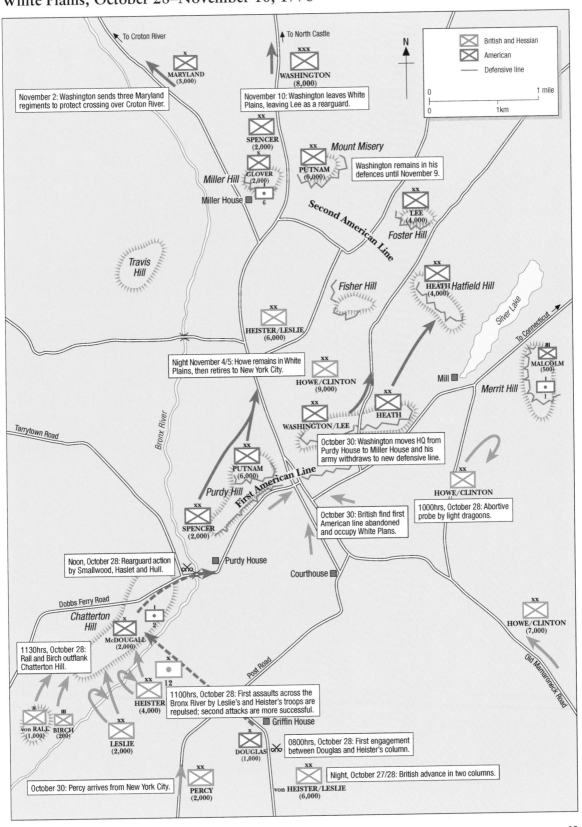

To Croton River

To North Castle

N

British and Hessian
American
Defensive line

0   1 mile
0   1km

MARYLAND (3,000)

November 2: Washington sends three Maryland regiments to protect crossing over Croton River.

WASHINGTON (8,000)

November 10: Washington leaves White Plains, leaving Lee as a rearguard.

SPENCER (2,000)

GLOVER (2,000)

Miller Hill

Miller House   6

PUTNAM (6,000)   Mount Misery

Washington remains in his defences until November 9.

LEE (4,000)

Foster Hill

Travis Hill

HEATH (4,000)   Hatfield Hill

Fisher Hill

Silver Lake

To Connecticut

HEISTER/LESLIE (6,000)

MALCOLM (500)

1

Night November 4/5: Howe remains in White Plains, then retires to New York City.

HOWE/CLINTON (9,000)

Merrit Hill

Mill

Tarrytown Road

WASHINGTON/LEE

HEATH

October 30: Washington moves HQ from Purdy House to Miller House and his army withdraws to new defensive line.

Bronx River

PUTNAM (6,000)

First American Line

HOWE/CLINTON

Purdy Hill

SPENCER (2,000)

October 30: British find first American line abandoned and occupy White Plans.

1000hrs, October 28: Abortive probe by light dragoons.

Noon, October 28: Rearguard action by Smallwood, Haslet and Hull.

Purdy House

Courthouse

Dobbs Ferry Road

Chatterton Hill

2

McDOUGALL (2,000)

HOWE/CLINTON (7,000)

1130hrs, October 28: Rall and Birch outflank Chatterton Hill.

12

HEISTER (4,000)

1100hrs, October 28: First assaults across the Bronx River by Leslie's and Heister's troops are repulsed; second attacks are more successful.

Post Road

Old Mamaroneck Road

von RALL (1,000)

BIRCH (200)

LESLIE (2,000)

Griffin House

DOUGLAS (1,000)

0800hrs, October 28: First engagement between Douglas and Heister's column.

October 30: Percy arrives from New York City.

PERCY (2,000)

von HEISTER/LESLIE (6,000)

Night, October 27/28: British advance in two columns.

More positively, Washington had regained the services of some of his most valued officers. Charles Lee had returned from Charleston (basking in the glory of the successful defense of Clinton's expedition earlier in the year even though he had played little part in it), while Sullivan and Stirling, captured at Long Island, had been exchanged. Lee's first action seems to have been to impress upon Washington the dangers of remaining at Harlem Heights, in which case he was entirely correct even taking into account Howe's ponderous progress.

This took another twist on October 18 when Howe, having wasted days at Throg's Neck, re-embarked his troops and moved them to the superior landing place at Pell's Point. The delay had given the Americans time to anticipate the move and a force of around 1,000 men under Colonel John Glover had been hurried to the spot to oppose a landing. Lord Stirling was advancing quickly from Harlem Heights with his brigade to secure the ground at White Plains where Washington intended to move his army.

Once more the contest had taken on the characteristics of a race. If the British could land, brush aside Glover's defenders and move out quickly, they could intercept Washington's main column, now numbering only around 13,000, and possibly destroy it. The day started well for the British, who landed 4,000 men before sunrise and were already pressing inland when Glover led 750 of his men to oppose them. Seriously outnumbered (and the situation only got worse for Glover as the British reinforced) he nevertheless managed to stage a magnificent defensive action that completely stalled the British advance. Having bought an extra day for the main army, Glover's men withdrew, having suffered only 21 casualties against an estimated 200–800 losses among the British and Hessians. The race was not yet over, however, and the next day Howe moved his army to New Rochelle and ordered his supplies to be sent there by ship. The British were now reinforced by a further division of Hessians, under Lieutenant-General Wilhelm von Knyphausen (awaiting the arrival of the Hessians was the main reason for Howe's delay in moving), which gave time for Stirling's advance party to secure the high ground at White Plains at 0900hrs on October 21.

Rufus Putnam, who had been ordered to scout out the British position and had communicated their proximity to White Plains to Washington and then Stirling, was amazed at Howe's lack of urgency. "I may be asked wherein this particular interposition of providence appears," he commented. "I answer, first, in the stupidity of the British general, in that he did not early on the morning of the 20th send a detachment and take possession of the post and stores at Whiteplains, for had he done this, we must then have fought him on his own terms, and such disadvantageous terms on our part, as humanly speaking must have proved our overthrow."

Howe was certainly not stupid, but his agonizingly slow progress was once more letting a chance for a decisive victory melt away. Henry Clinton was furious that his own plan for a much earlier landing at New Rochelle had been ignored. He rightly pointed out in his memoirs that such a move, undertaken when he had first advised it, would have put the Americans in a disastrous position.

Washington was now able to face Howe from yet another prepared defensive position, with about equal numbers. A line of hills to the rear of the village of White Plains offered a strong position and Washington aligned his troops along them. On the extreme right of his line, Chatterton Hill was cut off from the remainder of his forces by the Bronx River, isolating it and making it a questionable position to hold, but realizing that it was within artillery range of his right flank he decided it had to be garrisoned. He ordered around 1,000 men under McDougall to occupy the hill.

The British plan was once more not entirely to Clinton's liking. He had suggested yet another of his outflanking marches, again under the cover of darkness, but Howe preferred a more direct attack. He did, however agree with Clinton that separate columns should be employed and that the right column, commanded by Clinton, should attempt to get around Washington's left flank.

The British commenced their advance on the night of October 27/28 and when their approach was detected Washington sent out a force of around 1,000 men (from Spencer's Division and led by Douglas) to delay the advance of the combined British and Hessian column. Under Alexander Leslie and von Heister, this column included the 2nd Brigade and three Hessian regiments and numbered around 6,000. The two forces clashed at around 0800hrs. With the Americans was Tallmadge:

> At the dawn of day, the Hessian column advanced within musket shot of our troops, when a full discharge of musketry warned them of their danger. At first they fell back, but rallied again immediately, and the column of British troops having advanced upon our left, made it necessary to retire. As stone walls were frequent, our troops occasionally formed behind them, and poured a destructive fire into the Hessian ranks.

Only narrowly avoiding capture by the Hessians himself, Tallmadge and the rest of the advance force fell back to Chatterton Hill. Tallmadge immediately headed off to report to Washington.

On the British right, Clinton was finding it difficult to make any progress. "I was certain," he wrote, "the instant they discovered my column, they would retire; and I therefore halted the head of it and detached Lord Cornwallis from its rear with some battalions and cannon, with a view of getting around them." This plan was not able to be carried out before the Americans withdrew in the face of Clinton's advance, making this a frustrating morning for the British general. Nothing of any importance would happen on his flank.

Back at Chatterton Hill, a serious confrontation was developing. Leslie launched an impetuous charge up the slope of the hill and was met with a heavy fire from the American defenders—he was forced to withdraw with considerable losses. The American defenders were a mixture of some of the best men at Washington's command and some fairly unsteady militia. Haslet's Delawares and the remnants of Smallwood's Marylanders were there, alongside a two-gun battery under Captain Alexander Hamilton. With the men of Douglas' command the defenders numbered between 1,500 and 2,000. The Massachusetts Militia present had proved jittery from the start. A cannonball striking one of their number in the thigh had prompted an entire regiment to run, and although they had rallied they were nervous as the British and Hessians pressed the attack. By now attacking units had moved around the side of the hill and, charging up it, they caused the militia to break once more. The remainder of the defenders made a more organized withdrawal and the fighting for the day was over.

Howe declined to continue with his assault, possibly believing the American defenses to be stronger than they really were (in most cases they

THE ACTION AT SPLIT ROCK, OCTOBER 18, 1776 (pp. 72–73)

Washington's delay in removing his army from the Harlem Heights might have proved disastrous were it not for the success of a small American force under Colonel John Glover. British and Hessian troops had landed in force at Pell's Point and were marching to take possession of the high ground at White Plains along Split Rock Road. **(1)**.

Glover, with 1,000 men, moved quickly to intercept the 4,000-strong British force. First encountering the British advance guard, Glover sent 40 men to hold them up until he could prepare a defensive position.

The stone walls on each side of the road **(2)** were an obvious defensive structure that Glover determined to use. Positioning three of his four regiments behind the walls he kept a fourth, along with his artillery, on a hill overlooking the field of battle.

As the main body of British caught up with their advance guard the small delaying force before them was withdrawn and the British advanced quickly, thinking their way was clear.

Glover's first regiment now rose and delivered a powerful volley into the head of the advancing column, which was pressed tight in the road between the two stone walls. Retreating in confusion, the British and Hessian troops regrouped, were joined by reinforcements and advanced once more, this time under a covering barrage from seven field pieces.

Glover's men rose once more and exchanged volleys with the enemy (Glover reported seven rounds were fired at this point) before the first regiment withdrew and moved back along the wall, taking up a new position at the end of the concealed American line.

Again advancing quickly, the British were now assaulted by volleys from Glover's second regiment. Firing in "grand divisions," the Americans were able to keep the British at bay and inflicted serious casualties, forcing them to retreat **(3)**. A private in Colonel William Shepherd's regiment vaulted the wall at one point and removed a hat and canteen from a badly injured British officer **(4)**. The officer, Captain Evelyn of the 4th Foot, would later die from his wounds, having refused to have his right leg amputated until it was too late.

Curiously, the British made no effort to use their superior numbers to outflank their opponents, apparently thinking the battle was over each time a group of Americans withdrew. Eventually, weight of numbers told and Glover was forced to withdraw, having lost remarkably few men (he estimated eight dead and 13 wounded) while the British and Hessians lost anywhere between 200 and 800 dead and wounded (exact numbers are impossible to determine as William Howe never included Hessian casualties in his figures and the Germans bore the brunt of the fighting in this engagement). More importantly, the British advance towards White Plains had been stalled.

The action at Fort Washington is shown here in great detail, with the landing of the combined Cornwallis–Mathew force to the left and the Hessians advancing on the right. Just above the Hessians can be seen the *Pearl*, operating on the Hudson. (I. N. Phelps Stokes Collection, Miriam and Ira D. Wallach Division of Art, Prints and Photographs, The New York Public Library, Astor, Lenox and Tilden Foundations)

were merely uprooted corn stalks with the roots piled up to face the enemy and covered with earth—they probably looked formidable from a distance. As it was, Howe had paid a steep price to move the Americans from a single hill. His men had performed bravely (even an American officer commented on the charge of Leslie's men, saying that "It was a gallant sight to see them, steadily, without a falter, march up a very steep hill, exposed to a constant fire of cannon and musketry, until they attained the summit") but they had lost at least 200 men, compared with around 175 Americans. Howe settled for an artillery duel for the rest of the day and awaited further reinforcements.

Percy joined him from New York on October 30, with fresh units of Hessians and a Waldeck regiment. The intention was to attack again the following day, but severe rain made this impossible and by the time the weather cleared, Washington had withdrawn his entire army to a much stronger second line at North Castle Heights. Howe would not attack him there and the two armies simply faced each other for a few days. The increasing cold was a warning that the campaigning season was drawing to a close. The British lit large numbers of fires at White Plains to keep warm, while Joseph Plumb Martin wrote of frost covering the ground in the mornings. Howe now appeared seriously to doubt that he would be able to bring Washington to a major battle, noting that the American general seemed unwilling to stand unless he had strong defenses. On November 5, Howe returned to Manhattan.

FORT WASHINGTON

The isolated garrison at Fort Washington would be Howe's next objective, although this decision, like many of Howe's during the campaign, was questionable. When writing to Germain he pointed out that, in conjunction with Fort Lee, it commanded the Hudson River, which had been conclusively disproved on several occasions. The garrison was also too small to do anything but defend and could easily have been watched by a small number of British troops, freeing the bulk of the army to pursue Washington.

When Howe withdrew from White Plains the American commander-in-chief had made his now familiar mistake of dividing his forces in an attempt to cover all possible eventualities. Charles Lee was left at North

THE FUSILIER REGIMENT VON LOSSBERG AT WHITE PLAINS, OCTOBER 28, 1776 (pp. 76–77)

Chatterton Hill, forming Washington's right flank at White Plains, was an isolated and vulnerable position and an obvious target for Howe to move against. The British general sent the 2nd Brigade and three regiments of Hessians, including the Fusilier Regiment von Lossberg, to take the hill.

In order to advance on the hill, the British and Hessian troops first had to ford the Bronx River (1). The British did so quickly and began to taunt the slower-moving Hessians, who were crossing at a fairly deep point (one of their colour bearers was almost drowned in the crossing) under fire from the Americans defending the hill. Two British regiments made an impetuous attack on the hill but were beaten back.

Moving into a meadow of waist-high grass leading up to the hill, the Hessians advanced with a line of skirmishers (flanquers) to the fore (2). The grass was alight in several places, the result of burning wadding from the rifles of American skirmishers, and the Hessians held their cartridge cases high to avoid any chance of the gunpowder catching fire (3).

Soaked to the waist from their river crossing, their progress was slow and uncomfortable, and a burning wood on the left of the Hessian advance presented a serious obstacle, causing minor injuries to many solders as they passed through (4).

The American defenders were a mixture of disciplined units and jittery militia, but they stood firm while the Hessians advanced. The severity of the defending fire can be judged by the fact that the staff of the colonel's colour was smashed by grapeshot as it was carried forward by an ensign, with several others in the colour party and colour guard being struck at the same time (5).

Though criticized at the time by the British for the slowness of their advance, the Hessians pressed forward doggedly under the guidance of their officers (6) and advanced up the hill. Reports of the battle disagree and it is uncertain if they were repulsed but, if they were, they certainly returned to the attack. The critical moment of the action came when two Hessian regiments, under von Rall and von Knyphausen, together with some of the 17th Light Dragoons, attacked the Americans in their right flank and forced them to withdraw.

Hessian losses in the assault were three dead and 47 wounded and Washington's defensive line was now seriously compromised—Chatterton Hill could be used to site artillery that could rake the remaining American positions, but Howe would once more prove unwilling to prosecute a potentially decisive advantage.

Castle Heights with 7,000 men, 2,000 went with Washington to link up with 3,500 under Greene at Fort Lee (in case Philadelphia was the next target for the British) and 4,000 under Heath were sent up the Hudson to Peekskill to defend the Highlands. "This dispersion," in Mackesy's words, "meant weakness everywhere."

Washington had learned that a major battle was something to be avoided. "We should on all occasions avoid a general action," he had written before White Plains, "or put anything to the risk, unless compelled by a necessity into which we ought never to be drawn."

Howe was perhaps underestimating the value of Washington as a symbol of the revolution. By turning attention to Fort Washington, undoubtedly a soft target, he was removing his focus from the commander-in-chief, the capture or death of whom would have been a far more severe blow to the rebels' cause than the loss of a fort. Plans were already in motion, however. Von Knyphausen had been sent from New Rochelle to Kingsbridge before White Plains, arriving on November 2. Now the rest of the army joined them and a major assault was planned.

The British and Hessians would be attacking the same strong defensive works that had deterred Howe earlier in the year, on the Harlem Heights. The difference now was that the commander at Fort Washington, Colonel Robert Magaw, did not have anywhere near enough men to make full use of them. There was still time to evacuate and Washington was certainly in favor of this. He wrote to Greene, the main advocate of holding the fort and personally present at Fort Washington, on November 8, saying: "If we can not prevent vessels passing up, and the enemy are possessed of the surrounding country, what valuable purpose can it answer to hold a post from which the expected benefit can not be had?" Washington went on to say: "… as you are on the spot, [I] leave it to you to give such orders as to evacuating Mount Washington as you judge best." This could be read in two ways. Either Washington was leaving the decision of whether or not to evacuate the fort in Greene's hands, or he was ordering an evacuation and merely leaving the *details* up to Greene.

Greene replied, showing a remarkable lack of judgment. "I cannot conceive the garrison to be in any great danger," he wrote, "the men can be brought off at any time." He was by now aware of British designs on the fort: "I was over there last evening; the enemy seems to be disposing matters to besiege the place, but Colonel Magaw thinks it will take them till December expires before they can carry it."

The comforting presence of Fort Lee, on the other side of the Hudson, may have created the impression that an easy line of retreat was open, and Greene and Magaw might even have taken note of Howe's reluctance to assault prepared defenses. For whatever reason, the garrison remained.

Howe would show no reluctance to attack this time. He prepared a detailed plan, aiming to hit the Americans from three directions at the same time with overwhelming force. The idea was to drive them from their outlying

Being taken as a prisoner in the War of Independence could mean a bleak fate. Officers were routinely exchanged, but privates might end their days on prison hulks like the *Jersey*, where disease and starvation claimed hundreds of lives. (LOC, LC-USZ62-124949)

FORT WASHINGTON, NOVEMBER 16, 1776

Washington had left almost 3,000 men and a large amount of supplies at Fort Washington. Deciding against an evacuation, he trusted that the garrison would be able to hold out or inflict heavy casualties when Howe decided to take the fort following the action at White Plains

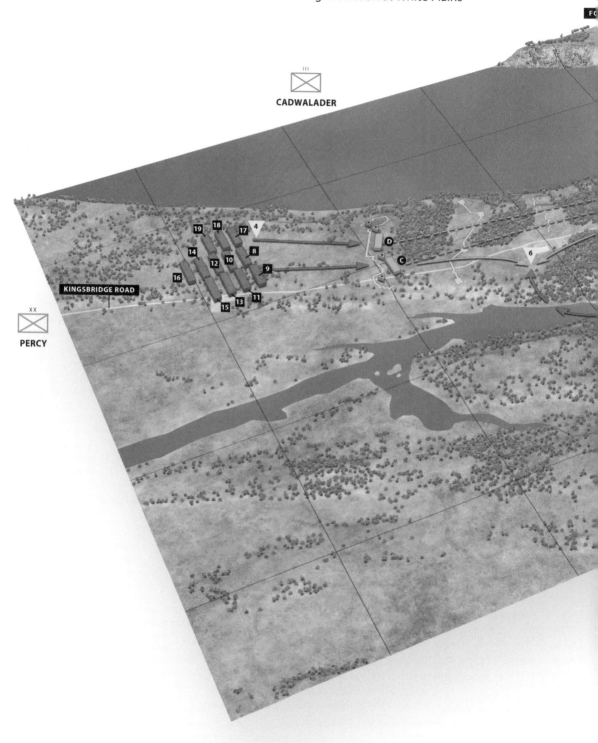

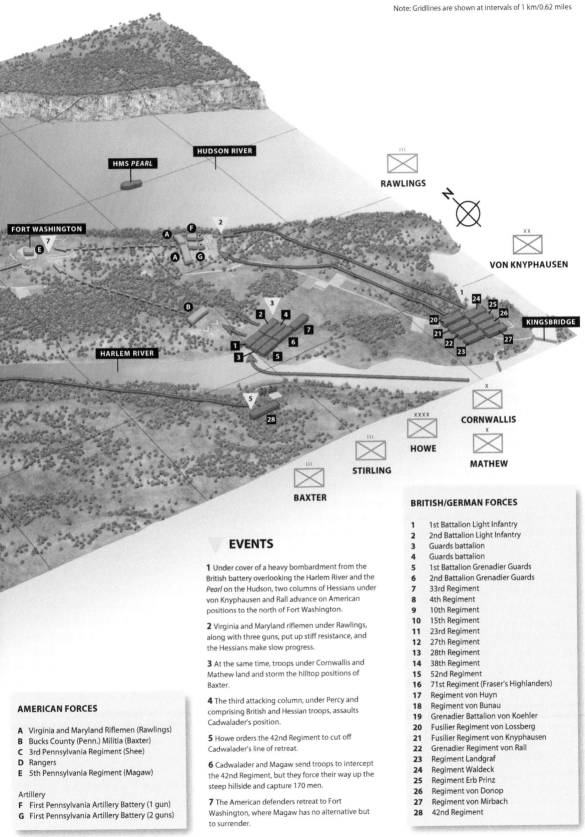

HUDSON RIVER

HMS *PEARL*

RAWLINGS

VON KNYPHAUSEN

FORT WASHINGTON

KINGSBRIDGE

HARLEM RIVER

CORNWALLIS

HOWE

MATHEW

STIRLING

BAXTER

EVENTS

1 Under cover of a heavy bombardment from the British battery overlooking the Harlem River and the *Pearl* on the Hudson, two columns of Hessians under von Knyphausen and Rall advance on American positions to the north of Fort Washington.

2 Virginia and Maryland riflemen under Rawlings, along with three guns, put up stiff resistance, and the Hessians make slow progress.

3 At the same time, troops under Cornwallis and Mathew land and storm the hilltop positions of Baxter.

4 The third attacking column, under Percy and comprising British and Hessian troops, assaults Cadwalader's position.

5 Howe orders the 42nd Regiment to cut off Cadwalader's line of retreat.

6 Cadwalader and Magaw send troops to intercept the 42nd Regiment, but they force their way up the steep hillside and capture 170 men.

7 The American defenders retreat to Fort Washington, where Magaw has no alternative but to surrender.

AMERICAN FORCES

A Virginia and Maryland Riflemen (Rawlings)
B Bucks County (Penn.) Militia (Baxter)
C 3rd Pennsylvania Regiment (Shee)
D Rangers
E 5th Pennsylvania Regiment (Magaw)

Artillery
F First Pennsylvania Artillery Battery (1 gun)
G First Pennsylvania Artillery Battery (2 guns)

BRITISH/GERMAN FORCES

1   1st Battalion Light Infantry
2   2nd Battalion Light Infantry
3   Guards battalion
4   Guards battalion
5   1st Battalion Grenadier Guards
6   2nd Battalion Grenadier Guards
7   33rd Regiment
8   4th Regiment
9   10th Regiment
10 15th Regiment
11 23rd Regiment
12 27th Regiment
13 28th Regiment
14 38th Regiment
15 52nd Regiment
16 71st Regiment (Fraser's Highlanders)
17 Regiment von Huyn
18 Regiment von Bunau
19 Grenadier Battalion von Koehler
20 Fusilier Regiment von Lossberg
21 Fusilier Regiment von Knyphausen
22 Grenadier Regiment von Rall
23 Regiment Landgraf
24 Regiment Waldeck
25 Regiment Erb Prinz
26 Regiment von Donop
27 Regiment von Mirbach
28 42nd Regiment

fortifications before they could make full use of them. Von Knyphausen would attack from the north, moving up from Kingsbridge with a force of Hessians. British troops under Cornwallis and Mathew would make a landing from the Harlem River and attack in parallel with von Knyphausen. At the south side of the defenses, Percy would lead two columns—one British and one Hessian—against the triple line of defensive works that Washington's men had constructed in September. The *Pearl*, on the Hudson, would bombard American positions while guns on the Fordham Heights would cover the landing of Cornwallis and Mathew.

To defend against this, Magaw posted Colonel William Baxter's Bucks County (Penn.) Militia at the north end of Laurel Hill, looking toward the British emplacements on the Fordham Heights. On the other side of the island, Colonel Moses Rawlings lined his Maryland and Virginia riflemen up at a redoubt at the tip of Mount Washington, facing where the Hessians would attack. Lieutenant-Colonel Lambert Cadwalader commanded Shee's 3rd Pennsylvania Regiment and the Rangers at the southern end of the defenses. Magaw's own 5th Pennsylvania Regiment completed the garrison of the fort. Three guns of the First Pennsylvania Artillery were also with Rawlings.

On November 14, Washington arrived and found that Greene had not evacuated the fort. Not for the first time, Washington acted slowly when faced with irrefutable evidence of danger. In the same way that he had delayed evacuating New York City and the Harlem Heights, he now delayed making a decision at Fort Washington. "His Excellency General Washington has been with me several days," wrote Greene. "The evacuation or reinforcement of Fort Washington was under consideration, but finally nothing concluded on." Washington had escaped unscathed from the predicaments at New York and the Harlem Heights, helped in no small part by Howe's slowness to act. Here he would not be so lucky and the failure to pursue either course—reinforce the fort to make it defensible, or withdraw the inadequate garrison immediately—deserves harsh criticism.

On November 15 Howe gave the garrison a chance to surrender, hinting that he would put them to the sword if they forced him to attack. Howe, of

course, had no such intention (although it was considered legal in the 18th century for an attacking force to vent their frustrations on defenders who had forced them to storm a fort or city). Nor did Magaw seriously intend to defend the fort "to the last extremity" as his defiant reply claimed. This was merely the rhetoric of the day and Howe actually gave the Americans a full night to consider the wisdom of staying put, ignoring the two-hour deadline he had issued. Washington ignored this last opportunity to do the sensible thing and bring his men across to Fort Lee and on November 16 he, together with Greene and other officers, crossed over to Fort Washington, in Greene's words: "to determine what was best to be done."

The decision was already out of Washington's hands. The three attacking columns advanced at almost the same time, with the Hessians having the toughest going. The hill in front of them was so steep they were forced to drag themselves up by holding onto bushes and their losses were heavy. Von

Washington's retreat, November 16–December 13, 1776

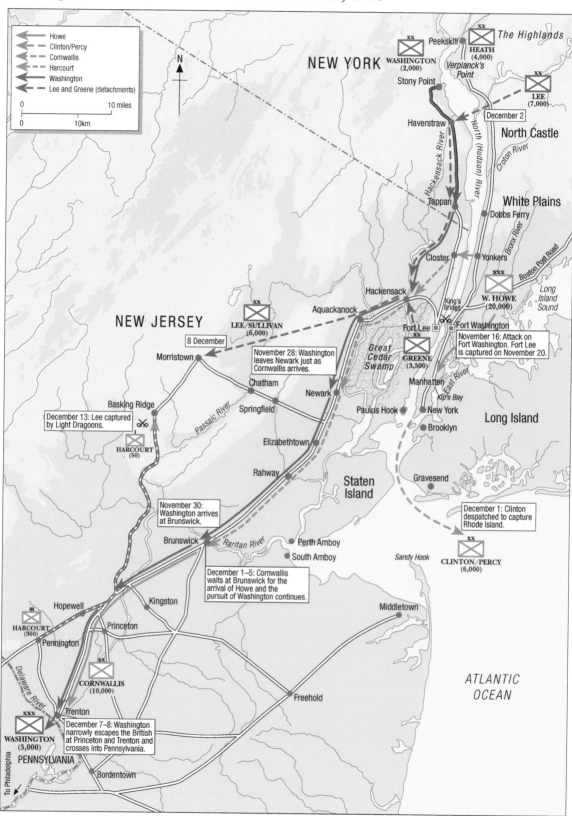

Legend:
- Howe
- Clinton/Percy
- Cornwallis
- Harcourt
- Washington
- Lee and Greene (detachments)

0 — 10 miles
0 — 10km

N

The Highlands

HEATH (4,000)
Peekskill
WASHINGTON (2,000)
NEW YORK
Verplanck's Point
Stony Point
LEE (7,000)
Haverstraw
December 2
North Castle
North (Hudson) River
Croton River
Hackensack River
Tappan
White Plains
Dobbs Ferry
Bronx River
Closter
Yonkers
Boston Post Road
Hackensack
W. HOWE (20,000)
Long Island Sound
Aquackanock
King's Bridge
Fort Lee
Fort Washington

LEE/SULLIVAN (6,000)
NEW JERSEY
8 December

November 16: Attack on Fort Washington. Fort Lee is captured on November 20.

November 28: Washington leaves Newark just as Cornwallis arrives.

Morristown
Chatham
Newark
GREENE (3,500)
Manhattan
Kip's Bay
East River
Basking Ridge
Springfield
Paulus Hook
New York
December 13: Lee captured by Light Dragoons.
HARCOURT (50)
Passaic River
Elizabethtown
Brooklyn
Long Island
Rahway
Gravesend
Staten Island

November 30: Washington arrives at Brunswick.

December 1: Clinton despatched to capture Rhode Island.

Brunswick
Raritan River
Perth Amboy
South Amboy
Sandy Hook
CLINTON/PERCY (6,000)

December 1–5: Cornwallis waits at Brunswick for the arrival of Howe and the pursuit of Washington continues.

Hopewell
Kingston
Middletown
HARCOURT (300)
Princeton
Pennington
ATLANTIC OCEAN
Delaware River
CORNWALLIS (10,000)
Freehold
WASHINGTON (5,000)
Trenton
December 7–8: Washington narrowly escapes the British at Princeton and Trenton and crosses into Pennsylvania.
PENNSYLVANIA
Bordentown
To Philadelphia

Rall and von Knyphausen led by example, von Knyphausen, despite his age, tearing at obstructions with his bare hands. The Guards had stormed Laurel Hill, putting Baxter's men to flight and killing Baxter himself while, to the south, Cadwalader's men began to buckle. Howe now sent in a fourth attacking party—the 42nd Regiment and two supporting battalions—to cut off Cadwalader's retreat to the fort. A detachment of about 250 men from both Magaw and Cadwalader was moved to intercept the Black Watch, but they climbed the steep hill at their landing place with such speed they took 170 prisoners.

From all quarters the American defenders moved back to the fort, which was not nearly big enough to accommodate them all safely. The attackers closed in and there is evidence that the Hessians, who had suffered the most in the assault, wanted to be let loose against the garrison. Instead, Magaw was invited to surrender and, having no alternative, he did.

Howe had shown a dashing and ruthless side that had been absent on so many other days in this campaign. Where at Brooklyn he had spurned an assault on American defenses because he thought the cost would be too high and the prize could be won "at a very cheap rate by regular approaches," at Fort Washington he boldly attacked, losing around 450 men and inflicting only around 150 casualties. The remainder of the garrison, however, was now taken prisoner.

Nathaniel Greene has generally taken the blame for persuading Washington to hold on to Fort Washington, but the commander-in-chief had the opportunity to evacuate on November 14, when he arrived, and again during the night of November 15, when the British ultimatum had been made. As the attack raged he even sent a message over to Magaw asking him to attempt to hold out until nightfall, when an attempt could be made to evacuate, an order that is rather ridiculous given the strength of the force moving against the fort. Greene himself was "mad, vexed, sick and sorry," as he wrote to Knox the day after the fall of Fort Washington, and he revealed his fear of blame in a heartfelt plea to his friend: "This is a most terrible event; its consequences are justly to be dreaded. Pray, what is said upon the occasion?"

Charles Lee's lackadaisical progress toward a link-up with Washington came to an abrupt end when he was captured by a British patrol including a young British cornet, Banastre Tarleton, at Basking Ridge, New Jersey. (LOC, LC-USZ62-45309)

The loss of Fort Washington was inexplicably followed up by the capture of a huge amount of supplies and ordnance at Fort Lee four days later. With Howe ordering Cornwallis and 6,000 men to pursue Washington through New Jersey, a landing was made upriver from Fort Lee and the garrison fled. Why a more timely and organized retreat had not been arranged after the fall of Fort Washington is a mystery. Between the two forts the Americans lost 146 cannons, 2,800 muskets and something like 400,000 cartridges. It was a staggering blow for an army already reeling.

Worse for Washington, Cornwallis proved to be far more energetic in his pursuit than Howe, once covering 20 miles in a single day in his effort to get at Washington's dwindling army, now numbering around 3,500 men. Washington sent orders for Charles Lee to join him but Lee's actions (he headed towards Washington at a leisurely pace) led some to believe he actually wanted Washington to fail so that he might be installed as commander-in-chief. He was too leisurely, as it turned out, being captured by a patrol of light dragoons on December 13, but he did have legitimate complaints. He had, he stated in a letter to Horatio Gates "neither guides, cavalry, medicines, money, shoes or stockings."

Howe had curiously ordered Cornwallis to pursue Washington no farther than New Brunswick, where the British commander-in-chief joined him, restarting the pursuit at Howe's more familiar pace. A spell of good weather temporarily gave Howe hope that he might capture Philadelphia before ending operations, a success that would have made a strikingly symbolic end to the campaign, but he eventually settled for driving Washington over the Delaware and out of New Jersey.

Clinton, on December 1, had been dispatched to take Rhode Island, an order that achieved the double aim of securing a good harbor for Admiral Howe's ships for the winter and getting the abrasive general out of William Howe's hair. The New York campaign was over and George Washington's Main Army was in tatters, having finally been reduced to running for its very existence away from the state it had determined to hold. New York was lost, almost 4,500 officers and men had been captured, with around 600 killed or wounded. Many more had simply walked away from the cause, some on the expiration of their enlistments, others unauthorized at various points in the campaign when the hardships had seemed too much to bear and the chances of victory too remote to consider seriously. Congress had moved from Philadelphia to Baltimore.

In short, the British Army had gone wherever it wanted, whenever it wanted. William Howe had been slow—puzzlingly slow at times—but the final result could hardly be argued with. There was just the one niggling concern—that Washington had escaped and still had the core of an army with him. Sir William Howe could not have guessed how serious that was to prove as the newly knighted general retired to New York to enjoy a winter's rest.

THE AFTERMATH

Judgment of William Howe's performance in the New York campaign of 1776 tends to be harsh, focusing on his failure to beat Washington's army decisively. Howe claimed to be seeking a major battle early in the campaign, but his actions repeatedly suggested otherwise and his protestations that he was chiefly concerned with limiting his own casualties can only excuse him so far—taking casualties in a single battle that would destroy the Main Army and potentially end the rebellion must have been preferable to prolonging the war and losing small amounts of men in repeated minor engagements. This was just the scenario many military authorities had dreaded, the destruction of the army "by damned driblets."

However, Howe is being judged with the benefit of hindsight and as things stood at the end of December the revolution might confidently have been expected simply to wither away in the harsh winter months to come. Washington's tiny remaining force was in rags, poorly supplied and bereft of almost all its artillery. Enthusiasm for the war was waning fast and Howe had ambitious plans to end the whole thing in 1777—if there was an army left to fight, that is.

His letter to Germain on November 30 outlined a devastating campaign. An army of 10,000 men, under Clinton, would operate offensively from Rhode Island, moving on Boston and possibly taking it. Another 10,000 men would move from New York and take the offensive along the Hudson. A defensive force of 8,000 would remain in New Jersey and would then take Philadelphia in the autumn, before moving into Virginia. South Carolina and Georgia would be the targets for a winter campaign. With garrisons of 2,000 men for Rhode Island and 5,000 for New York, Howe's total numbers

This familiar-looking view of New York is a copy of the Howdell image of 1768 (see page 58, published as it was in November 1776, it now depicts massed ranks of British soldiers on the island of Manhattan. (LOC, LC-USZ62-45417)

This cartoon, in which a British officer demonstrates to two cowering Native Americans the power of Britain's military forces, has an ironic twist. Its text refers to fighting between Howe and Washington on September 19, 1777—the day when the war started to go irretrievably wrong for the British at Saratoga. (LOC, LC-USZ62-5219)

BELOW, RIGHT
Washington crosses the Delaware and prepares to strike a blow that will reignite the revolutionary cause at Trenton. (LOC, LC-USZ62-5850)

would need to be 35,000—and he accordingly asked Germain for 15,000 reinforcements. Given the huge problems Britain had faced in getting Howe's army of 25,000 in place for the 1776 campaign, this request was simply unreasonable and Germain's reply, on January 14, 1777, included a frank admission from the Colonial Secretary that he had been "really alarmed" by it. Germain hoped that something like 7,000 reinforcements might be found.

Before Germain sent this reply, Howe had already written again with a change of plan. On December 20 he stated that he now intended to open the 1777 campaign by taking Philadelphia, because he believed Pennsylvania was ready to submit to British authority. The shift of emphasis meant the bulk of his troops, 10,000, would now be used in Pennsylvania. Until his requested reinforcements arrived the garrisons at Rhode Island and New York (now estimated at 2,000 and 4,000 respectively) would act on the defensive. Only 3,000 men would be allocated to move on the Hudson under this new plan, "to facilitate in some degree the approach of the Army from Canada."

This was a major shift away from the Hudson strategy and it occurred even before Washington shocked the British by mounting daring and successful raids on Trenton and Princeton. New life was breathed into the

Princeton quickly follows Trenton and Washington has proved that his army is far from finished. The two victories are small, but hugely important at the same time. (LOC, LC-USZ62-2774)

revolutionary cause and an entirely different complexion was put on the 1776 campaign. News of Trenton reached Germain in March and he wrote to Howe that it was "extremely mortifying." He also felt the need to impress upon Howe the fact that more harsh measures might be needed for the following year: "I fear that you and Lord Howe will find it necessary to adopt such modes of carrying on the war, that the Rebels may be effectually distressed, so that through a lively experience of losses and sufferings, they may be brought as soon as possible to a proper sense of their duty." In other words, it was time to stop treating them so gently. Germain also gave his approval to Howe's revised plan, which is curious considering it seriously undermined the Hudson strategy.

The strategy was to be undermined further when Howe received Germain's answer to his request for 15,000 reinforcements. Howe's reply to Germain on April 2 has a distinctly peevish tone and he had changed his plan once more. New Jersey would have to be abandoned and he would be forced to take the offensive in Pennsylvania by sea. Only a force of provincials under Governor Tryon would be employed on the Hudson, a force that Howe admitted would be "too weak for rapid success." Operations would start later than planned because of the need to evacuate New Jersey and "… any hopes of terminating the war this year are vanished."

On April 5 Howe wrote to Carleton, informing him that he would not be able to detach a force up the Hudson. In fact, as he would be in Pennsylvania, he would not even be able to communicate easily with the Canada Army. It would therefore be up to Carleton (or, as it turned out, John Burgoyne) to do what he thought was best.

The Hudson strategy had been abandoned. Germain gave no orders to Howe to insist on support for Burgoyne as he moved south, yet the Canada Army went ahead with its push southward. The result was the defeat of Burgoyne at Saratoga and the first decisive victory of the war. Having had the chance to secure one for the British so many times in the New York campaign of 1776, Howe's actions in 1777 had contributed to the loss of an entire British Army. With the defeat of Burgoyne, the French felt able to support the American rebels openly and the war entered a new phase. It would effectively end with the capture of the British Army under Cornwallis at Yorktown, in 1781, although it dragged on for two more years following this.

The surrender of Burgoyne at Saratoga was not only the first major victory for the Americans, it gave France all the encouragement it needed to pick up its old argument with Britain officially and turn what had been a "family affair" into a world war. (LOC, LC-USZ62-186)

BELOW, RIGHT
Washington's triumphant re-entry into New York on November 25, 1783, was a fitting end to a war that had begun in earnest in the same city seven years previously. (LOC, LC-USZ62-3915)

New York would play a relatively minor role for the remainder of the war and the British would hold it until 1783, when they finally set sail for home. On November 25, 1783, George Washington entered the city he had lost seven years previously on the heels of the evacuating British, and the moment was captured perfectly by an eyewitness:

> The troops just leaving us were as if equipped for show, and with their scarlet uniforms and burnished arms, made a brilliant display. The troops that marched in, on the contrary, were ill-clad and weather-beaten, and made a forlorn appearance. But then they were our troops, and as I looked at them, and thought upon all they had done for us, my heart and my eyes were full, and I admired and gloried in them the more because they were weather-beaten and forlorn.

THE BATTLEFIELD TODAY

LONG ISLAND

The massive building work undertaken on Long Island in the last two centuries has gone a long way to destroying the landscape of the biggest battle of the American War of Independence. The destruction started almost immediately, when the British leveled Cobble Hill after forcing the Americans to retreat to Manhattan. Other hills have been flattened and the earth used to fill in the marshes at Gowanus Creek and Wallabout Bay, changing the very dimensions of the island.

Barnet Schecter, in his book *The Battle for New York*, laments that New York did not remain the capital city of the United States, as it became in 1789, because then more might have been done to preserve the landscape of this important confrontation. Still, tantalizing glimpses of the old lie of the land can be found at Greenwood Cemetery, Prospect Park and the Cemetery of the Evergreens, which collectively mark out the line of the old Gowanus Heights along which the American advanced positions were located. Greenwood Cemetery is home to Battle Hill, Battle Pass is to be found in Prospect Park

The Cortelyou House, reconstructed and relocated, is one of the highlights of the battlefield at Long Island. (LOC, HABS NY, 24-BROK,40-2)

and the route of the British flanking march goes through the Cemetery of the Evergreens, giving three intriguing snapshots of the battle. Schecter gives a detailed description of a bus and walking tour of the battlefield that takes in these three key sites on the website detailed below.

The site of the heaviest fighting of the day, the Cortelyou House, has been reconstructed, although it has also been relocated a block from its original position. Also known as the Old Stone House, it is easy to imagine musket fire pouring from the windows as Lord Stirling mounted his brave but doomed holding action. The house contains exhibits depicting the Battle of Long Island and can also be booked for tours and classes. (The house also served as clubhouse for the Brooklyn Dodgers, making this site of special interest to those who combine an interest in military history with a love of baseball).

One of the few actual monuments to the war is to be found in Fort Greene Park (actually the former site of Fort Putnam). The Prison Ship Martyrs' Monument remembers the hundreds of American prisoners of war who died in squalid conditions while in captivity.

MANHATTAN AND NEW JERSEY

Fort Washington is no more, although its commanding position can still be experienced in Fort Washington Park. A glance across the Hudson also reveals the site of Fort Lee. Quarter of a mile from there is Fort Lee Historic Park, which features mock gun emplacements and a reconstruction of 18th-century buildings. The two-storey visitor centre includes a wealth of information on Washington's retreat across New Jersey as well as detailed dioramas, including one of the British landing at the Palisades. The Visitor Centre is open from Wednesday to Sunday, 1000–1700hrs, March to December.

USEFUL WEBSITES

Revolutionary War Road Trips www.revolutionaryday.com
The Old Stone House Historical Organization www.theoldstonehouse.org
The Battle for New York Walking Tour www.thebattlefornewyork.com

BIBLIOGRAPHY

MANUSCRIPT SOURCES

Egerton Manuscripts, British Library, London: 2135—Original letters and papers relating to military and naval operations in North America and the West Indies; 1762–95.

The National Archives of the UK, at Kew, Surrey, are home to a huge amount of documentation relating to the War of Independence. Of particular interest to this book are: Military Dispatches: (TNA): PRO CO 5/92 (1774–75), (TNA): PRO CO 5/93 (1775–76), (TNA): PRO CO 5/94 (1776–77), (TNA): PRO CO 5/95 (1777–78).

PUBLISHED PRIMARY SOURCES

Cumming, W. P. and Rankin, H., eds., *The Fate of a Nation: The American Revolution Through Contemporary Eyes* (London: Phaidon Press, 1975)

Fortescue, Sir J., ed., *Correspondence of King George III, Vol. III, July 1773–December 1777* (London: MacMillan and Co., 1928)

Gruber, I. D., ed., *John Peebles' American War, 1776–1782* (Stroud: Army Records Society, 1998)

Howe, W., *The Narrative of Lieut. Gen. Sir William Howe, in a Committee of the House of Commons, on the 29th of April, 1779, Relative to his Conduct, During his Late Command of the King's Troops in North America* (London: H. Baldwin, 1780, Second Edition)

Rhodehamel, J., ed., *Writings* (New York: The Library of America, 1987)

Scheer, G. F., ed., *Private Yankee Doodle: A Narrative of some of the Adventures, Dangers and Sufferings of a Revolutionary Soldier* (Boston: Little, Brown and Company, 1962)

Seybolt, R. F., ed., "A Contemporary British Account of General Sir William Howe's Military Operations in 1777," *American Antiquarian Society* (April, 1930), pp. 74–76

Stevens, B. F., ed., *General Sir William Howe's Orderly Book, 1775–1776* (London: B.F. Stevens and Brown, 1890)

Tallmadge, B., *Memoir of Colonel Benjamin Tallmadge* (New York: New York Times & Arno Press, 1968)

Willcox, W. B., ed., *The American Rebellion: Sir Henry Clinton's Narrative* (New Haven: Yale University Press, 1954)

Wright, E., *The Fire of Liberty* (London: The Folio Society, 1983)

SECONDARY SOURCES

Bicheno, H., *Rebels and Redcoats* (London: HarperCollins, 2003) One of the liveliest and most original modern considerations of the War of Independence.

Black, J., *Warfare in the Eighteenth Century* (London: Cassell, 1999)

Black, J., *War For America: The Fight for Independence, 1775–1783* (Stroud: Sutton Publishing Limited, 2001)

Boatner, M., ed., The Encyclopedia of the American Revolution (Mechanicsburg: Stackpole Books, 1994)

Burrows, E. and Wallace, M., *Gotham: A History of New York City to 1898* (New York: Oxford University Press, 1999) Invaluable for putting the War of Independence, and the role played by New York, into perspective.

Conway, S., *The War of American Independence 1775–1783* (London: Edward Arnold, 1995)

Curtis, E., *The Organization of the British Army in the American Revolution* (Yale: Yale University Press, 1926) Also available as a Scholar's Bookshelf reprint edition (2005)

Chartrand, R., Elite 93: *American War of Independence Commanders* (Oxford: Osprey Publishing 2003)

Fortescue, Sir J., *The War of Independence: The British Army in North America, 1775–1783* (London: Greenhill Books, 2001)

French, D., *The British Way in Warfare 1688–2000* (London: Unwin Hyman, 1990)

Greene, J. P. and Pole, J. R., eds., *The Blackwell Encyclopedia of the American Revolution* (Oxford: Blackwell Publishers, 1991)

Gruber, I. D., *The Howe Brothers and the American Revolution* (New York: Atheneum, 1972)

Johnston, H. P., *The Campaign of 1776 Around New York and Brooklyn* (New Jersey: Scholar's Bookshelf, 2005) Originally published in 1878, this is a detailed and valuable account of the New York campaign and comes with three excellent battlefield maps and a wealth of original documents.

Lefferts, C., *Uniforms of the American, British, French and German Armies of the War of the American Revolution* (Old Greenwich: W.E. Inc. Publishers 1976) This book not only contains many beautiful paintings by Charles M. Lefferts, it also includes exhaustive detail on uniforms and some useful unit histories.

Lowell, E. J., *The Hessians and the other German Auxiliaries of Great Britain in the Revolutionary War* (New York: Harper and Brothers, 1884) Unusual in its focus on the Hessians, this provides invaluable detail on the provision of German troops.

Mackesy, P., *The War for America: 1775–1783* (London: University of Nebraska, 1993)

May, R., Men-at-Arms 39: *The British Army in North America 1775–83* (Oxford: Osprey Publishing 1997)

Milsop, J., Warrior 68: *Continental Infantryman of the American Revolution* (Oxford, Osprey Publishing 2004) Includes detailed photographs of an enormous number of weapons used in the war.

Neumann, G. *The History of the Weapons of the American Revolution* (New York: Harper and Row 1967)

Sabine, H. W., *Murder, 1776 & Washington's Policy of Silence* (New York: Theo. Gaus' Sons, 1973)

Schecter, B., *The Battle for New York* (London: Jonathan Cape, 2003)

Underdal, S. J., ed., *Military History of the American Revolution* (Washington: Office of Air Force History, 1976)

Weintraub, S., *Iron Tears: Rebellion in America, 1775–1783* (London, Simon & Schuster 2005) Offers very useful insight into the political situation in Britain.

ARTICLES

Black, J., 'Eighteenth-Century Warfare Reconsidered', *War in History*, 2 (2) (1995), pp. 215–32

Conway, S., 'Britain and the Impact of the American War, 1775–1783', *War in History*, 2 (2) (1995), pp. 127–50

Conway, S., 'British Army Officers and the American War for Independence', *The William and Mary Quarterly*, 41 (2) (Apr 1984), pp. 265–76

Gruber, I. D., 'Lord Howe and Lord George Germain: British Politics and the Winning of American Independence', *The William and Mary Quarterly*, 22 (2) (Apr. 1965), pp. 225–43

Seymour, W., 'Turning Point at Saratoga', *Military History*, 16 (Dec 1999), p. 46

Willcox, W. B., 'British Strategy in America, 1778', *The Journal of Modern History*, 19 (2) (1947), pp. 97–121

INDEX

Figures in **bold** refer to illustrations.